Heaven
Calling

365 Day Devotional

STEPHEN VAN ZANT

Heaven Calling

365 Day Devotional

FAITH FOR TODAY

REDEMPTION PRESS

Published by Redemption Press, PO Box 427, Enumclaw, WA 98022

Toll Free (844) 2REDEEM (273-3336)

Redemption Press is honored to present this title in partnership with the author. The views expressed or implied in this work are those of the author. Redemption Press provides our imprint seal representing design excellence, creative content, and high quality production.

All Scripture quotations, unless otherwise indicated, are taken from the *Holy Bible, New International Version*®. *NIV*®. Copyright © 1973, 1978, 1984 by International Bible Society. Used by permission of Zondervan. All rights reserved.

Contemporary English Version (CEV) Copyright © 1995 by American Bible Society.

God's Word Translation (GW) Copyright © 1995 by God's Word to the Nations. Used by permission of Baker Publishing Group.

Good News Translation (GNT) Copyright © 1992 by American Bible Society.

Jubilee Bible 2000 (JUB) Copyright © 2000, 2001, 2010 by Life Sentence Publishing, Inc.

English Standard Version (ESV) The Holy Bible, English Standard Version. ESV® Text Edition: 2016. Copyright © 2001 by Crossway Bibles, a publishing ministry of Good News Publishers.

The Message (MSG) Copyright © 1993, 1994, 1995, 1996, 2000, 2001, 2002 by Eugene H. Peterson.

New American Standard Bible (NASB) Copyright © 1960, 1962, 1963, 1968, 1971, 1972, 1973, 1975, 1995 by The Lockman Foundation.

New King James Version (NKJV) Scripture taken from the New King James Version®. Copyright © 1982 by Thomas Nelson. Used by permission. All rights reserved.

New Living Translation (NLT) Holy Bible, New Living Translation, copyright © 1996, 2004, 2007, 2013, 2015 by Tyndale House Foundation. Used by permission of Tyndale House Publishers Inc., Carol Stream, Illinois 60188. All rights reserved.

World English Bible (WEB) Public Domain.

O Jesus, I Have Promised Public Domain.

ISBN 13: 978-1-68314-609-4 (Paperback)
978-1-68314-610-0 (ePub)
978-1-68314-611-7 (Mobi)

Library of Congress Catalog Card Number: 2018933417

O Jesus, I Have Promised

O Jesus, I have promised to serve Thee to the end;
Be Thou forever near me, my Master and my Friend;
I shall not fear the battle if Thou are by my side,
Nor wander from the pathway if Thou wilt be my Guide.

O let me feel Thee near me, the world is ever near;
I see the sights that dazzle, the tempting sounds I hear;
My foes are ever near me, around me and within;
But, Jesus, draw Thou nearer and shield my soul from sin.

O let me hear Thee speaking in accents clear and still,
Above the storms of passion, the murmurs of self-will;
O speak to reassure me, to hasten or control;
O speak, and make me listen, Thou Guardian of my soul.

O Jesus, Thou has promised to all who follow Thee,
That where Thou are in glory there shall thy servant be.
And Jesus, I have promised to serve Thee to the end;
O give me grace to follow, my Master and my Friend.

John Ernest Bode, 1816–1874

Foreword

IN THE AUTUMN of 1986, my mother gave me a copy of the devotional *God Calling*. Two poor women, who referred to themselves as the Two Listeners, wrote the book in the 1930s in England. At the time, I was entering my first year of college at the University of Kentucky. I was not a religious person, and my family had not been regular churchgoers. However, this devotional had a curious effect on me as its simple messages of love, joy, and peace drew me in.

Four years later, I became a Christian while in my first year of law school at the University of Louisville. I believe *God Calling* planted the seeds of faith I needed to discover the Jesus of the New Testament. In January of 2004, fourteen years after my baptism, I happen to reread the foreword to *God Calling* and noticed for the first time the reference to the book *For Sinners Only* by A. J. Russell. I soon obtained a copy for myself, and Mr. Russell's description of an assembly of Christians known as the Oxford Group intrigued me. This group tried to imitate first-century Christianity and practiced the spiritual discipline of quiet listening. My wife and I began to practice quiet listening, or two-way prayer, in our own quiet times and found in it an added sense of joy, peace, and insight in our morning devotionals.

Some may doubt our ability to hear His voice today; others may find the whole practice of quiet listening a form of heresy. I can only speak of my own experiences, which have shown me that He is willing to deliver needed spiritual messages and practical insight to personal problems daily. This book is a compilation of my entries over the past fourteen years as recorded in twenty-three journals. These entries were never meant to be made public; it has only been recently that I felt prompted to put them together in a book formatted like *God Calling*. It is my hope that this devotional may encourage you and provide greater faith in His specific plan for your life. It is not necessary that it prompt you to try the practice of quiet listening, although I hope it will. (See afterword: "Suggestions for Quiet Listening.")

God Calling may be the inspiration for this book, but this devotional is different in several respects. The amount of prayer *from* the Two Listeners in *God Calling* is limited; in *Heaven Calling*, I provide more of my daily prayers. Often, I discovered that when I was experiencing the greatest stress, my journal entries had greater meaning. Proverbs 17:28 states, "Even fools are thought wise if they keep silent, and discerning if they hold their tongue." Similarly, Mark Twain once said, "It is better to keep your mouth shut and appear a fool, than to open it and remove all doubt." By publishing this book, I risk not following this advice by including my private prayers and by sharing the content of the entries themselves.

The entries included in this devotional reveal my daily personal struggle to find peace and joy. I do not claim to have experienced more problems than others have. In fact, I think the entry from July 3 is correct in stating, "Life is difficult for everyone." The words of C. S. Lewis also ring true that "most of us hold our mental health by a thread." In this regard, I suppose I have had my fair share of problems and personal trials through twenty-six years of marriage, raising four children, experiencing family health issues, practicing law, and suffering a business failure. I have heard that the best advice when traveling is to observe new surroundings with a sense of appreciation instead of comparison.

I think the same advice works well in considering the struggles of others.

Another area where this work differs from *God Calling* is the number of times there are promptings to repeat brief prayers or short sayings. *God Calling* contains some of these. For example, it suggests "All is well" many times as a wise refrain. The entries in this book contain a larger number of these short prayers. When compiling this devotional, the number of times I had written, "Pray today," or "Say today" struck me. For instance, the entry for March 31 suggests that I say, "Jesus guides my way," September 17 implores, "God bids me to rest," October 11 encourages, "The real me rests with Jesus," and October 13 states, "Let love prompt all I do or say."

Many of my journal entries have a different feel to them than those in *God Calling*. I find the entries in *God Calling* to be beautifully written and pleasant to read. When I review the entries in *Heaven Calling*, I think they, too, convey the gentleness of Jesus, but many also contain a directness that differs from the entries in *God Calling*. The Bible tells us that Jesus is the same yesterday, today, and forever. However, what we need from Jesus and how we need to hear it is different for each of us. Likewise, Paul's letters to Timothy are different in tone and content than his letter to Titus. Paul was the same, but the personalities and needs of Timothy and Titus were far different. Similarly, in Acts 2, the Jews all heard the Good News in their *own* language. I believe Jesus speaks to us in the way that is most beneficial for us to hear, though He himself never changes.

There are numerous references in *Heaven Calling* to the masculine gender. I have received suggestions that by shifting to gender-neutral wording, this book might find a wider audience. Since I never intended these entries to be anything other than private, I did not set out to make any type of patriarchal point by this language; I simply wrote as I heard. Some may say that this only shows that I am a product of my own environment. This may very well be true, but I hope the reader would understand my reluctance to change the language from how it was originally written, in part to keep this devotional as genuine as possible. Additionally, I believe that gender distinctions have value as we discover our spiritual identities as men and women of faith. For example, the consequences of Adam and Eve's fall as reflected in Genesis 3 are quite different for women than for men. Likewise, there are entries in *Heaven Calling*, like March 12, September 24, and October 8, where I wrestle with what it means to be a man of faith.

This is a book for the humble. It is for those who recognize that they are broken and in need of a Savior who has the power to renew them day by day. I do not claim to be an expert in matters of faith. I do not have a degree from a seminary and have never been on a church's staff. I certainly do not claim to have any special insight into the Christian faith. Moreover, I have a lot to learn about godliness and imitation of our great Friend. Accordingly, I offer this book as an amateur's collection of personal quiet times and in the spirit of "sharing my notes" with you. It is my great pleasure to sit with Him each morning and allow Him to change me. My prayer is that that this book may in some small way draw you closer to Him.

Stephen Van Zant
November 14, 2017
Crestwood, Kentucky

Spiritual Success

Lord, thank You this morning for refreshing my soul with the joy of spiritual growth. Give me a full portion of Your will to implement in my life. Let me feel the joy of helping others as You are helping me.

NEW BEGINNINGS BRING renewed hope for success. All true success is spiritual. Spiritual success may mean a new lesson learned, a new hope believed in, or a troubling sin overcome. It may mean finding new strength in Me. Make it your ambition to be a channel through which I can carry out My work, first within your own life, and then in the lives of others. Your spiritual success comes from continual surrender to Me. Know that only surrender to Me brings true hope, joy, and peace; tell others that only such a life truly lives well.

In the same way, those of you who do not give up everything you have cannot be my disciples. Luke 14:33

Sweetness to Christianity

Jesus, help me today to be strong in grace in my thoughts and actions.

LEARN TO VALUE My grace like my servant Paul, who had to turn from his obsession with following the letter of the law in order to find Me. Be true to the Word but closer to Me. The Word was meant to be understood through grace-filled eyes. My grace qualifies, completes, and satisfies you. Know no religion besides a grace-first, Spirit-led set of beliefs. Let My grace, peace, and calm fill you today. There is a sweetness to Christianity that no other philosophy can provide. It is the effect of grace.

For the law was given through Moses; grace and truth came through Jesus Christ. John 1:17

14 | Heaven Calling

Say Thank You

*I am sorry for the apprehension that I have allowed
to control me in the last few days. Restore calm in me.*

SAY YOUR THANK-YOUS to Me. Break through the clouds of despondency and despair with thanksgiving. Let the light of praise change the downcast morning and brighten the day. There is much to be thankful for. See and name the sources of joy all around you. This is My will for you today.

Rejoice always, pray continually, give thanks in all circumstances; for this is God's will for you in Christ Jesus. 1 Thessalonians 5:16–18

Relax and Trust My Protection

Lord, you know my struggles. I feel You have largely left me alone with the day-to-day pressures of my work and finances. Be big in my life. Overcome the evil one and this sense of failure.

YOU FEAR WHAT could go wrong in your life. You worry especially about finances. You seek safety and security, and I have pushed you out into deep waters. My command to you is relax and trust My protection. Feel protected and blessed. I will hold you safely from all threats—safer than the gold in Fort Knox. You stuff these worries within you in your waking hours, but I see them. Say today, "My Lord will protect me from all harm."

He that dwells in the secret place of the most High shall abide under the shadow of the Almighty. Psalm 91:1 JUB

JANUARY 5 —
Sunshine

Jesus, shed light on my day the way only You can.

IS THERE ANYTHING more beautiful than sunshine? Its rays bring clarity, life, and warmth. Imagine the earth without it: bleak, dark, and cold. The same is true for each man who lives without the light of Heaven. Let My light be in you. My light fills you with love, joy, and peace. My light makes your path clear. Brighten your day by keeping Me at the center of your being. Say to yourself, "I have Jesus' light within me."

Yet I am writing you a new command; its truth is seen in him and in you, because the darkness is passing and the true light is already shinning. 1 John 2:8

Competence

Thank You for all Your blessings; help me overcome my insecurities.

YOUR COMPETENCE SHOULD come from God. All men have different gifts and callings, but a man's fitness for each task comes from Me. This is a hard lesson for you. It is the Lord who completes you and enables you to carry on every good work. Can you see yourself as always competent to carry out any task I give you? See yourself as a capable servant for Me. I will show you the areas where you can help Me. Be an able minister, made competent by Me for the tasks I set before you. This competence comes from God the Father and Jesus your Lord.

Philip said, "Lord, show us the Father and that will be enough for us." John 14:8

Greet One Another Warmly

Use our family as you will.

LET ME HAVE full sway in your home. I love being here. Take My peace of mind when you have none of your own. Take My love for life when you have depleted your own supply. I will send others here for you to help. Greet each of them warmly. I can use you and each member of your family to encourage others.

Aquila and Priscilla greet you warmly in the Lord, and so does the church that meets at their house. 1 Corinthians 16:19

Calm in All Things

Lord, help me overcome this sense of dread.

HEAR MY VOICE tell you that "all is well." When you are afraid, draw back into the protection of your Lord's strong tower. When you have no particular command or request from Me, travel along the path I have set for you. Drown out the many voices that scream for your attention. Be calm in all things; this is the key to your success today. Calm in all things. It is a peace that comes from trusting Me.

In quietness and trust is your strength. Isaiah 30:15

JANUARY 9 —
False Religion

Lord, instill in me a full sense of sonship.

FALSE RELIGION IS rooted in performance instead of identity. It emphasizes what you do rather than who you are. Have a strong identity as a son of Our Father. All the good you can do in this life stems from this conviction. Be a warrior against false religion that judges you and leaves you feeling empty. The letter (the law) kills, but the Spirit gives life and encouragement. It is easy for men to fall into the performance trap. Understand the depth of Our Father's love. Accept your identity as firmly rooted in Him. Do not diminish your closeness to Him because of your shortcomings. Repent of performance-based religion. I have set you free from that, and if the Son has set you free, you are free indeed. Be Our Father's son in thought and deed.

For those who are led by the Spirit of God are the children of God. Romans 8:14

JANUARY 10 –

Jesus Calms Me

*Give me a softer heart so that I can have insight into
Your will.*

SAY TO YOURSELF, "Jesus calms me." Say it as a balm to a hurried mind. Say it as medicine to soothe aching nerves. Say it as a cheer to show others the path to peace. Live in the unrushed atmosphere of Heaven. Imitate My poise and calm. I always have plenty of time and can lead you down the right paths when you rest with Me.

Be still, and know that I am God. Psalm 46:10

JANUARY 11 –

The Father's Love

Jesus, please bless this sinner who loves You.

YOU SIT WITH pencil ready, a pure instrument because of My redeeming love. This morning, step aside from the earth's clocks and calendars. Move away from the things in the world you see. Come with Me to the precipice of eternity. Do you feel that? It is love's strong wave as it rushes around us. It is the Father's love. It travels from Heaven to earth to heal, encourage, and redeem. It is always searching, always looking for the heart that is ready to turn to Heaven. Your Father is love.

Whoever does not love does not know God, because God is love. 1 John 4:8

New Adventures

Lord, change me from the inside. Make me new and different. Help me to serve the kingdom better, in particular ways planned for me.

YOU ARE LIVING for eternity so you are always young. Your outlook should be youthful. I plan to do more with the rest of your life on this earth than I have with the first. Swelling up in your soul is a Heaven-planted desire for change. It is part of My way for My loved ones to sense this unrest for a time so they are prepared when I call them to new adventures. You have no idea where I am leading you; you only sense that change is coming to your life. All change from Me is a blessing.

"Come follow me," Jesus said, "and I will send you out to fish for people." Mark 1:17

Kicking against the Goads

Lord, have Your way.

SET YOUR AFFECTIONS on Me. Be at the center of My will for you. Be at the heart of what I want for you and your family. Self clamors to be first. Self wants to plan this day and every day. Self resists the flow of the Spirit throughout the day. When the self in you resists My Spirit, you are like the Sanhedrin, who opposed Peter and John. Gamaliel counseled them that they might be fighting against God. Likewise, I had to challenge Paul to stop kicking against the goads. Let that not happen with you. Be surrendered, not just now in your morning time with Me, but all day, every day. Some days you are a spiritual man in the morning but a secular man by the afternoon! Seek to stay a surrendered spiritual man all day.

We all fell to the ground, and I heard a voice saying to me in Aramaic, "Saul, Saul, why do you persecute me? It is hard for you to kick against the goads." Acts 26:14

The Blessed Road

God in glorious tripart, I give You thanks today for all—the good and the bad. Please forgive my worry and discontentment.

I AM HERE to help, here to save, here to direct. Walk in lockstep with Me as we march your path together: uphill, downhill, or straight and level. I choose the path, but we walk it together. The road may be dirt, gravel, or paved, but it will be glorious. Any road that you walk with Me is a road to glory. See yourself as blessed in every situation. Say to yourself today, "I am blessed."

Whether you turn to the right or to the left, your ears will hear a voice behind you, saying, "This is the way; walk in it." Isaiah 30:21

JANUARY 15 –
Physical Health

Lord, direct all my steps.

GUARD AGAINST TOO much activity today. You are still sick. Do all at the proper time. You need rest and healing. Spiritual health is often connected to physical health. Pray for physical healing to help you be closer to Me, to be better aware of My presence. Rest with Me as you recover. When you must interact with the world around you, have calm conversations. Say to yourself, "I am wrapped in His peace."

Dear friend, I pray that you may enjoy good health and that all may go well with you, even as your soul is getting along well. 3 John 2

JANUARY 16 –
Living for Eternity

Lord, help me find meaning in life today.

YOU ARE LIVING for eternity. Smile! No matter the issue, be absolutely unrushed and unhurried. Seek to find enjoyment in the day. Seek to find joy in every activity, knowing that I have worked out in advance all the details of every day. This creates the joy of childlike trust and joyful expectancy. Surely, I am with you to the end of the age (including today!). Plus, I give you the gift of eternity.

I give them eternal life, and they shall never perish; no one will snatch them out of my hand. John 10:28

Valley Irritations

Where are You, Lord, when trouble comes? Lord, where is Your protection when the evil one lurks?

THE PROBLEMS YOU face are smaller than you think. They are gnats and flies, valley irritations only. No disease or disability threatens your health. No evil attack has befallen you. Heaven is not removed from you—it is only hidden from your view. I taught My disciples on smooth mountain slopes filled with sunshine and warm air. Return there with Me now. Bow your head, and I will bless you.

Then Jesus went up on a mountainside and sat down with his disciples. John 6:3

Celebrate Me

Let me know Your will and give me the courage to obey it.

FIND THE JOY in life as you await My deliverance. I hear your prayer for change. You seek a different routine, the added joy of serving Me in a more rewarding way. Part of the discipline of following Me is trusting My timing. As you wait, there are always gifts for the day. Today is a good time to celebrate your salvation. Celebrate Me and the fact that you know Me and the power of My salvation for your life. This focus is your revival. The sky could fall, but you would still have Me, and your salvation would remain.

Praise be to the God and Father of our Lord Jesus Christ, who has blessed us in the heavenly realms with every spiritual blessing in Christ. Ephesians 1:3

Honest Sharing

Lord, show me Your excellent way.

COMMUNICATE THE VALUE of grace today instead of performance. Be ready to admit that you do not measure up to the man you wish to be. Let no facade hide others from the real you. Give yourself away by admitting mistakes. You draw others closer to yourself, and to Me, by honest sharing than by finely tuned speeches. Move others by your humility. In doing so, you show them that you trust more in grace than you do your own performance. Little by little, you learn what it means to live by grace.

Here is a trustworthy saying that deserves full acceptance: Christ Jesus came into the world to save sinners—of whom I am the worst. 1 Timothy 1:15

The Gift of Attention

Jesus, help me to impact the world for You.

SEE THE CONNECTION between giving attention and fully accepting others. Give the gift of attention to your family and others today. Enjoy being with them. Your preoccupation with your own thoughts, goals, and struggles limits your ability to encourage others. A person will feel full acceptance if they, in fact, have your full attention. Sometimes your sinful temptation is self-preoccupation. Let Me worry about you. Place your total focus on the other person, and then they will feel accepted and loved.

Accept one another, then, just as Christ accepted you, in order to bring praise to God. Romans 15:7

Jesus Is Warmth

Lord, thank You for a happy and warm home.

ON THIS COLD morning, you have warmth from the furnace. But, more importantly, you have warmth from above. The love of the Father through Me breaks the ice and warms the heart. All the houses on the street may be warm, but the hearts of many are cold. The world's chill on each heart can only be removed by My warm embrace. Embarrassments, personal failures, broken relationships—these cause man's heart to grow cold. And, a cold heart cannot warm another cold heart. Rejoice today that you know where to turn to restore your own heart with a warmth that comes from above and finds rest in your inner being, a warmth that spreads to your face and tells the world, "Jesus is warmth for all of us."

I will give you a new heart and put a new spirit in you; I will remove from you your heart of stone and give you a heart of flesh. Ezekiel 36:26

JANUARY 22 –

Spiritual Nourishment

You are enough for me today.

LET MY PEACE and contentment run through your veins. Let spiritual nourishment enrich your soul. As good food fuels a body's return to health, My spiritual nourishment allows the soul's return to well-being. The answers to the world's problems are spiritual. Say, "Jesus is spiritual health for me." Let faith win over doubts. Let heavenly patience fill your inner being. Let nothing ruffle your sense of peace and quiet in Me. Bow your head; let Me bless you.

This will bring health to your body and nourishment to your bones. Proverbs 3:8

The Health the Soul Craves

Lord, on days like these, I come before you empty and broken. You know my needs and mistakes. I look to You to rediscover joy and peace.

CANDY SUITS WHAT the body wants, but not what it needs. Empty calories provide only fading energy. Nature's fruit is healthy for the body. Healthy thinking is good for the soul. Wrong thinking brings heartache and sadness. Whether it is a misunderstood biblical principle or, what is more common, a wrong view of yourself, wrong thinking propels a downward spiral. It depletes you of light and life. Right thinking is like a healthy diet for your soul: it fuels energy and sustains life. Set your mind on Me by repeating My words to you, words of grace and worth, second chances, and new beginnings. Have a healthy mind by not focusing on the first thing that comes to you, but refocusing on what's better, what's gracious and kind. This is the health the soul craves. Keep a mind that rests in My grace, love, and patience.

Be careful how you think; your life is shaped by your thoughts. Proverbs 4:23 GNT

The Quick Obedience

Lord, I want to be one who walks all the way with You. Help me to have a faith that pleases You.

YOUR EFFORTS TO seek more and more of the Christian life are being rewarded. Always take the next prompted step. Let obedience be the hallmark of your faith. Out of My respect for man's free will, I do not force the change in each heart that I desire. Nor do I force My followers to obey My requests. Let your faith be a testament to the value of a surrendered will, the listening ear, and the quick obedience. As you listen, I speak to you. When you obey My commands, I can act. This is the promise of a beautiful faith.

You are my friends if you do what I command. John 15:14

JANUARY 25 —

Return to Me

Lord, come into my life in fuller measure.

IN THIS WORLD, you will have times when you feel far from Me. Doubt, busyness, sin, and other obstacles can separate you from Me. In these times—when you feel distant from Me—remember what you believed to be true when your faith was stronger. Today, use what you have learned to stay close to Me. Claiming that My will be done in a situation draws you closer to Me. Sharing about Me with others brings you closer to Me. Thanking Me for all the good you see pulls you closer to Me. Claim, share, thank. Do this continually. I am always here, but sometimes there are obstacles that prevent you realizing My presence. Your efforts to return to Me will be rewarded.

Immediately, something like scales fell from Saul's eyes, and he could see again. Acts 9:18

Let My Grace Rule Your Day!

Help me to continue to grow in grace.

YOU ARE STRONG in truth but weak in grace. You are improving in this area of your life but ever so slowly. I came in *grace* and truth. Let My grace rule your day! Love the good in everyone. It is far easier for you to find fault in yourself and others. Instead, have a new perspective. Say to others, "What I like about you is . . ." Think of each person you meet as a child of God. Every person falls short of Heaven's plans for them, but grace can come alongside them and make them whole. You see grace in an inferior manner. You cannot give grace to others until you receive it yourself. To give it fully, you must receive it fully. When you were still living in rebellion to Heaven, I came for you.

But God demonstrates his own love for us in this: While we were still sinners, Christ died for us. Romans 5:8

JANUARY 27 –
Guidance

Lord, thank you for Your rich mercy that allows me to walk with You each day.

WHEN THE TEMPLE'S curtain was torn in two, it demonstrated man's ability to return to God's presence. The power of My cross reestablished the ability for man to commune directly with Heaven's throne room. Here, with grace applied, I speak to you and give you the guidance you need, the injunctions for the big and small decisions in your life. New light is shed each day when you walk with Me in this way. Take My guidance and hold to it; it will helm your ship to safety and glory. Say to yourself today, "He has plans to give me hope." Submit gladly to Me, your kind King.

At that moment the curtain of the temple was torn in two from top to bottom. Matthew 27:51

Unselfish Living

Make me a fit instrument for Your use.

TRUE HAPPINESS IS found in living for Heaven and others and not for self. Selfish living brings bitterness and strife. Unselfish living reaps joy and freedom. Live for the other fellow; sense his needs and hurts. This is where I lead you. Pick what is best for the soul, not what suits the self. The clamor of the self is loud, persistent, and ends in ruin. Connect your soul with Me today and be gently led. Go where I call you. Let My sympathies become your sympathies.

An unfriendly person pursues selfish ends and against all sound judgment starts quarrels. Proverbs 18:1

JANUARY 29 —
Your Great Reward

Lord, I will not leave here until You bless me.

YOU COME HERE in humility, not pride. Your greatest strength is that you value what is spiritual. You know that you must come to Me each day for your spiritual needs. Search for Me every day with all your heart, and you will find all you could ever want. I am your great reward. Ask Me to stay with you all day.

So Jacob was left alone and a man wrestled with him till daybreak . . . But Jacob replied, "I will not let you go unless you bless me." Genesis 32:24, 26

A Free Child of God

Lord, free me from all that presses against me.

FEAR AND SHAME are the devil's tools, shackles to bind you in slavery. My intention is for you to be a free child of God. Fight fear and shame. Fight fear with childlike trust. Fight shame with praise to Heaven. Feel free to make your demands on Me. You are dearly loved, and nothing is too small to be discussed with Me. Nothing is too minor for which to seek My guidance. Bring Me all the enemy's chains; I am strong enough to break them. Together we conquer.

I have forgiven in the sight of Christ for your sake, in order that Satan might not outwit us. For we are are not unaware of his schemes. 1 Corinthians 2:10–11

JANUARY 31 –

Simplify

Lord, help me. I pray for a miracle in my heart. Remove from me all that is not part of Your plan.

IN THE MIDST of your struggles, I am here. In the height of despair, I have not budged. Earth's noises drown out My quiet voice. I wait, knowing that you will return to your spiritual senses. Make your day less complicated. Say no and simplify. One-voice living is your path to peace. One-Master obedience is your road to calm living. There are many things that you feel obligated to do. Keep close to Me, and I will clear away agitation and work not prompted by Me. Say, "I am content with Him alone."

"Martha, Martha," the Lord answered, "you are worried and upset about many things, but few things are needed—or indeed only one. Mary has chosen what is better, and it will not be taken away from her." Luke 10:41–42

My Gospel Is for Everyone

Jesus, teach me how to have a life that is in You today. Teach me where I need to die to self and where I can live for You.

MY GOSPEL IS for everyone. *Everyone* is one of the most inviting words in the English language. It's also a very Christian word. Everyone can turn to Me to be saved. Everyone can receive eternal life. My gospel is an equalizer that ignores race, color, class, and social standing. You follow a revolutionary—I want to save the whole world. My gospel is for everyone.

For there is no difference between Jew and Gentile— the same Lord is Lord of all and richly blesses all who call on him, for, "Everyone who calls on the name of the Lord will be saved." Romans 10:12–13

Sacrifice of Thanksgiving

Lord, save me from this dark mood I am in.

THE PARTS OF your character that are forged in intense heat will remain permanently. Your perseverance will outlast the pressures you face in this season and will be like treasure in Heaven that cannot be stolen. Set your mind on thanksgiving today. As you outlast your troubles, offer the sacrifice of thanksgiving to Me. It is a sacrifice because it is the opposite of what you feel like doing. The sacrifice of thanksgiving is a mighty tool to overcome the world and its downward pull on you. Use it powerfully and rejoice in the mettle being formed in your character.

For our light and momentary troubles are achieving for us an eternal glory that far outweighs them all. 2 Corinthians 4:17

Generous Listening

Thank You for this time with You; help me to wait patiently.

GENEROUS LISTENING BRINGS bright and clear direction. Cultivate silence with Me as you await your daily blessing. Understand My heartache when My followers bring me their problems and fail to wait for My comfort and My response. Little do they realize that all the comfort Heaven can provide is theirs, and all the wisdom Heaven contains is at their disposal. Yet, so few wait.

My dear brothers and sisters, take note of this: Everyone should be quick to listen, slow to speak and slow to become angry. James 1:19

FEBRUARY 4 —

Fresh Water

Lord, my faith and hope are low. Build me up as only You can and send me back out.

ONLY MY PRESENCE completes your soul and restores your faith and hope. Only contact with Me can remove the brine and impurities of this earth life. Only life with Me heals your brokenness. Only following Me sets you on My adventures. My plan is to fill your life with My fresh water and provide glad adventures to chase away the monotonous and mundane life. A chorus of angels cheer you on to success. Say to yourself today, "The Lord provides me with fresh water."

Indeed, the water I give them will become in them a spring of water welling up to eternal life. John 4:14

No Rush into the Kingdom

Lord, help me to be completely under the sway of the Holy Spirit. Help me to be responsive to Your leading.

ASK ME TO show you where I am working. Subtlety, heavenly pressure is being brought to bear on many around you to bring them closer to Me. Sense what I am trying to do in each life and work with Me. Follow where I guide you, but also wait when I bid you to be patient. You may plant the seed, and another may reap the harvest. There is no rush into the kingdom. What I plan as a person's next step toward Me may be different than what you think is needed. Only Heaven knows the complexity of each human heart and how best to heal its maladies. A student may leap overnight into the welcoming arms of the kingdom; an adult may take years to shed impediments to Heaven's call. Trust me to guide each soul back home; act when and how I prompt you.

When he had finished speaking, he said to Simon, "Put out into deep water, and let down the nets for a catch." Luke 5:4

Hear and Live

Lord, I feel like I am driving on ice-clad roads with no ability to stop or steer. I want to stop, but I careen ahead.

SEEK MY QUIET this morning. To be led by My Spirit, you must push back the parts of your day that rage for your attention. Be quiet so that you can hear and live. In this quiet, I can speak to you. My responses to your prayers can be drowned out by the racing thoughts that rush through your mind. Firm commitment to hearing Me is a discipline learned by practice. I am here with you. Trust not only My strength, but My ever-abiding presence.

Take my yoke upon you and learn from me, for I am gentle and humble in heart and you will find rest for your souls. Matthew 11:29

Notice the Simple Beauty

Lord, give me a heart that is like Yours.

THE ABILITY TO celebrate simple beauty is a trait you can learn from Me. Enhance your ability to notice it all around you, whether it is beauty in nature or beauty in a human soul. Watch others closely. There are plenty of beautiful acts of love and kindness that go unnoticed and unheralded. It was the widow's two small coins that drew My attention. Her generosity toward Heaven was unrecognized by the crowd. But, I saw her act and praised the heart that prompted it. It was the kind of generosity that reminded me of Our Father. I celebrated her beautiful giving. Be not only quick to listen, but quick to watch. By watchful living, you can see the beauty that abounds even in this troubled world.

Jesus sat down opposite the place where the offerings were put and watched the crowed putting their money into the temple treasury. Mark 12:41

The Joyous Life

Jesus, fill me with Your joy.

YOUR SUCCESS IS not a result of luck, intelligence, or hard work. Your success results from living in My presence and obeying My commands. This is the victory born from a life lived with Me. It is the success that demonstrates the wisdom of a surrendered life. It is a life that is not surrendered to the people or circumstances around you, but surrendered to Me and the joyous life I have planned for you. Surrendered living is a gift, first for yourself, then for those near you.

For whoever wants to save their life will lose it, but whoever loses their life for me will save it. Luke 9:24

Heavenly Adrenaline

Thank You for all good things. Thank You for continuing to work in the hearts of people.

THERE IS A joy to hearing My words to you and obeying what I have asked. You can then happily leave the result to me. However, there is added joy for My followers when they see Me work in the lives of others through their acts of obedience. This is the fruit that comes from submission. Together, we share in that joy along with all the citizens of Heaven. It is the rush of heavenly adrenaline, the hope that good things are still happening, and that I can still make all things new.

They asked each other, "Were not our hearts burning within us while he talked with us on the road and opened the Scriptures to us?" Luke 24:32

One Path to Peace

Jesus, I call on Your name for new life and direction.

LOVE THOSE WHO seek me vainly on wrong paths. Many are man's philosophies on this earth. Scratching and clawing, he yearns for satisfaction. He discovers that his contentment is difficult to find. He looks for the God he needs in money, a relationship, or an achievement. See the good in all who are on such errant paths. You have been on such paths yourself, and I loved you still. When the rich young man turned away from Me, I loved him. There is good in everyone because all are made in God's image. Love them and show them that there is one path to peace for man's soul. I am the universal bridge for all men. I am Jacob's ladder for all to reach the invisible God. I am the peace that transcends all logic.

Jesus looked at him and loved him. Mark 10:21

Closer to Heaven

Father, Son, and Spirit, thank You for Your rich blessings. Thank You that I can arise each day to be refreshed by You.

TRULY, THE CHRISTIAN life is the best life: accepted by the Father, loved by Me, and led by the Holy Spirit. Once that life has been tasted, who would go back to living without God? Grace is given to you to wash away yesterday's missteps and failures. I provide the true path to upward mobility. Each day that passes, you are closer to Heaven. Each day that passes, I work with you to bring more of Heaven to your life and character. Improvement to improvement, success to success, guidance to guidance. Closer to Heaven each day.

I have come that they may have life, and have it to the full. John 10:10

My War of Love

Give me guidance to obey when I'm feeling dull.

THE PRIVATE DOES not understand the whole war. He must trust his commander's knowledge and wisdom. Trust Me and the gentle instructions I give you. I see the whole picture of your life and everyone I long to save. Growth comes at the death of pride. In humility, trust Me with the simple errands I give you. You see the small daily events, but I put all the pieces together to wage My war on the earth, My war of love over hate, faith over fear, and of building up instead of tearing down. My war gathers people to Me and Heaven. The evil one longs to scatter men and women, leaving souls isolated and lonely. I need humble soldiers to wage My war together with Me.

The LORD is a warrior; the LORD is his name. Exodus 15:3

A Rewarding Life

Lead me today, Lord, where You will.

OH, WHAT A wonderful, rewarding life when all your efforts and pursuits are from and in Me. The simple joy of a guided life. In his heart, man fears that his life is without meaning, that the events in his life do not move him toward a worthy purpose. Feel the joy of knowing that I link your life with Heaven's aims. When you daily surrender your life to Me, I add rich meaning to your days. You do not have to worry about planning your future. I, your good Master, am doing that for you.

Always give yourselves fully to the work of the Lord, because you know that your labor in the Lord is not in vain. 1 Corinthians 15:58

The King of Kings

Thank You for Your sacrifices for me and the grace You have made available.

PURPLE IS THE color of royalty—its rare shade reserved for earth's wealthy and powerful. The Christ you follow is not weakened or defeated. You serve a God who wins, a God who never stumbles or despairs. I, your King, continue to serve man. I came to show man a new majesty, a majesty that seeks to serve. When I was on earth, the soldiers believed they mocked a failed man who led a lost cause. They saw Me as a delusional philosopher. Little did they know that the King of kings sat before them, outwardly beaten and bruised, but inwardly triumphant, faultless, and pure. Before them sat a King more powerful than they could imagine, a King who could have called twelve legions of angels to His defense. Inwardly, I knew the completion of Our Father's dream was close at hand. Today the world sees a weak and helpless Christ. Together here with Me, you see that My kingdom is strong to save. Its influence still changes the world one soul at a time. Even today, the King of kings is ever sending His tender communion invitation to each soul, ever extending His royal hand to each person.

They put a purple robe on him, then twisted together a crown of thorns and set it on him. Mark 15:17

My Timing Is Perfect

Lord, do not delay in fulfilling Your promises.

SO MANY OF My lessons for you point toward the joy of a surrendered life. My timing is perfect. Would you rush it? I will provide. I hold eternity in My hands and can best plan your life. I urge My followers to humble themselves under My protection and guidance. Walk with Me on the path I have set for you. Leave the details of the turns, terrains, and vistas to Me. You have the power to ruin the joy of each day when you yearn for something different than what I have planned. Find joy in the life you have now.

The Lord is not slow in keeping his promise, as some understand slowness. 2 Peter 3:9

Continual Rescues

Lord, my heart is heavy. Yesterday, I made mistakes.

I SPECIALIZE IN continual rescues—that is why I came to earth. My ways to save you are creative. They are uniquely designed for you. There is a beauty to My creative saving power that is often unrecognized. My sheep wander down wrong paths; they are enticed to dangerous places. They use their freedom to walk into slavery. I, your Good Shepherd, am strong to save, but also strong to keep. When you wander, I gently bring you back to where you should be, where you will find rest. When you are too weak to walk back, I place you on My shoulders. I am strong enough to keep you.

I am the good shepherd. The good shepherd lays down his life for the sheep. John 10:11

A Changed Life Tells

Thank You for these dark woods I see. Help me to understand Your mysteries.

I WANT YOU to feel My love and acceptance. I want you to trust My protection as you live under the shadow of My wing. Many of My followers talk to others about Me without projecting any joy from being near Me. Their words sound hollow and do not hit the mark. Genuineness can be gauged even by a small child. To convince others that I am the Way, the miracles I perform in your heart must be apparent to others. A smile from one encouraged deeply within shines brightly for all to see. A gentle touch from one who has been accepted by Me has its effect. The welcome from one who no longer walks alone is inviting. Medicine offered by one who has been made well is wanted. A changed life tells.

But Zacchaeus stood up and said to the Lord, "Look, Lord! Here and now I give half of my possessions to the poor, and if I have cheated anybody out of anything, I will pay back four times the amount." Luke 19:8

Pray about All Things

Jesus, I pray for Your order in my life. I sense a spirit of disorder within me. Help me to be responsive to Your leading.

YOU ARE LEARNING that I have not called you to do all things, but only those things I prompt you to do. However, you can pray about everything. It is the duty of My believers to offer up prayers for change when they see hurt and pain in the lives of others. You can work powerfully through your day by prayer when you lift your concerns to Heaven's listening ear. Unless I prompt you to act, your duty is finished. When Peter led the lame and sick to Me outside his mother-in-law's home, I had to tell him that soul starvation was My concern for that day. This did not mean I was unsympathetic to those hurting and that I did not lift their needs to the Father. Believe in the power of Heaven to set all things right. Speak to Me often; act as I prompt you.

Jesus replied, "Let us go somewhere else—to the near-by villages—so I can preach there also. That is why I have come." Mark 1:38

My Constant Presence

Lord, thank You and praise You for the secret joy and peace that You alone can provide.

MAN WAS CREATED to live in unbroken accord with his God—God-guided, God-directed, and God-protected. To lose this was man's fall from grace and his shame. Be full of faith, full of belief in My constant presence as it was in the beginning. I defeated sin so you would not need to hide from Me. You will remain broken until you leave earth, but unbroken accord is possible here and now by the power given to you by My grace. Say to yourself, "My powerful Friend is here."

Then the man and his wife heard the sound of the LORD God as he was walking in the garden in the cool of the day, and they hid from the LORD God among the trees of the garden. Genesis 3:8

Light Always Overcomes Darkness

Lord, be close to me when life offers little joy.

LET MY LIGHT break through again in your life. My light always overcomes darkness. Giving thanks to Me allows My light to shine in your life. If your road feels dark, sing praises to Me. If you need a starting point, focus on My creation all around you. In all seasons, there are wonders to behold. See My creative beauty no matter the season. Even in the bleak of winter, My beauty surrounds you. When you cannot see it, let faith in My goodness propel you forward. When the dark seems impenetrable, know that it will fade with the light of My dawn.

For since the creation of the world God's invisible qualities—his eternal power and divine nature—have been clearly seen, being understood from what has been made, so that people are without excuse. Romans 1:20

The Gift of a Heavenly Perspective

Jesus, thank You for meeting me without fail every day.

OFTEN, MY FOLLOWERS stumble through life without a heavenly perspective. In this earth life, your worries and fears loom large and feel insurmountable. From Heaven's perspective, they are light and momentary. They can be reduced to faint whispers and small tremblings. Thus, you see the need for this daily time with Me. Each man needs time to change his perspective, to see life from above, far above the pangs and pulls of this earth life. Together with Me, your problems become smaller, and the might of Heaven becomes larger. Today I give you the gift of a heavenly perspective.

I lift up my eyes to the mountains—where does my help come from? My help comes from the LORD, the Maker of heaven and earth. Psalm 121:1–2

Your Very Personality

Come, Lord Jesus. Have Your way in my life and in the world around me. Help my life be one You can be proud of.

LET MY LOVE and grace to you not be without effect. Let your very personality be bent by Heaven's many spiritual currents. Be strong and very courageous. Be more childlike and playful in person. Be unswervingly obedient to My commands because of your love for Me. Take on the dignity of one serving a King. Have the eternal peace of one whose home is with Me. These are all heavenly currents molding you to be the man you were intended to be. See the value in adding goodness to the world over a lifetime. Compare this with a lifetime ravaged by sin and darkness.

But by the grace of God I am what I am, and his grace to me was not without effect. 1 Corinthians 15:10

FEBRUARY 23 –
Spiritual Fullness

Jesus, thank You for teaching me to seek Your presence and that this brings You joy. Thank You for enjoying me.

BEING CONSCIOUS OF Me is simply being aware of the truth of My presence in your life. Speak to me more to be made aware of My closeness. My dear ones know that I love them but often do not believe that I enjoy being with them. I enjoy being with you and hearing from you. Speak to Me more during the day. Speak to others when guided by Me. It is then that we speak together. Speak to Me in sentences and paragraphs within the silence of your own heart. In this way you will be filled with My spiritual fullness for you. Too much talk by you drains the emotional fullness I would have for you.

A good man brings good things out of the good stored up in his heart, and an evil man brings evil out of the evil stored up in his heart. For the mouth speaks what the heart is full of. Luke 6:45

When You Are Ill

Lord, help me to feel better.

BY RESTING, YOU serve Me by gathering strength for tomorrow. However, you can have My joy in full measure today despite being physically sick. Sometimes when you are ill, you can have an even better day spiritually. Since you are more aware of your need for strength, you walk closer with Me. Say, "I can do all things through Him who sustains me." Then, do less and allow Me to do more. Pray more and leave the details to Me.

Come to me, all you who are weary and burdened, and I will give you rest. Matthew 11:28

Heavenly Interruptions

Jesus, give me peace of mind in the midst of this busy life.

DELIBERATE TIME SPENT alone with Me is the key to overcoming the haste and feverous pace of modern life. Here you are reminded that you are living for eternity. You learn the poise that only eternal life can provide. On earth I was resolute in My path to the cross but not so rigid that I failed to see the needs of those around me. Adherence to a rigid path hinders kingdom work. I grant peace and even a leisurely pace to My dear ones. See in My life on earth that there was no hurry. There was no rush in My interactions with others. My opportunities for you often appear as interruptions. When walking to heal Jairus' daughter, I was not bothered by the interruption of the woman who had suffered with hemorrhage. There was no busyness to My pace when I was interrupted by the pleas from blind men. My life on earth was not My own, but I wanted the good and pleasing will of the Father to be done. And, so with you. Gladly submit your will to Mine. When the interruptions come, accept them as heavenly interruptions warmly sent by Me. Gladly accept Heaven's interruptions in your day. Be available and attentive.

Therefore, as we have opportunity, let us do good to all people, especially to those who belong to the family of believers. Galatians 6:10

The Kingdom Advances

Whether in a small or large way, Lord, use me.

YOU CANNOT CONTROL the wind, but you can have your sails up and catch it when it comes. Be ready! Be alert! The glory of the kingdom of God is that it is continually advancing: fight to fight, person to person, soul to soul, deep talk to deep talk. God looks for the places where He can gather lost souls and return them to a state untainted by sin. My tender communion is offered to all. If a thousand things cause a man to turn to Me, he may be aware of only a few. The orchestration of his turning, the battles that raged in the spirit world, may go unobserved. Be ready to do your part in this fight, to be put in place to fight kingdom battles. It is to this glorious work that My followers have been called.

He answered them and said, "The kingdom of God does not come with observation; nor will they say, 'See here!' or 'See there!' For indeed, the kingdom of God is within you." Luke 17:20–21 NKJV

I Am Being Blessed

Lord, I do not see the reason for this trial, but I trust Your care for me.

LET TRUST IN Me rinse away agitation and worry. Let simple but firm trust in Me be a hallmark of your life. See yourself as blessed in every situation. Say to yourself today, "I am being blessed." To every interruption, every trial, every telephone call, say, "I am being blessed." Rid yourself of this feeling of dread that forces are working against you. Trust that your kind Lord cares deeply for you and is leading you in a wonderful way.

And God is able to bless you abundantly, so that in all things at all times, having all that you need, you will abound in every good work. 2 Corinthians 9:8

May Your Kingdom Come

Please give me quiet in You so that I can find life.

YOUR FIRST TASK today, as every day, is to push back all that comes rushing at you. Push back the earth demands that clamor for your attention: the mundane, the selfish, the emergencies. Push those back and say to yourself, "May my kingdom go and Your kingdom come." Each day, start by seeking My kingdom in terms of Heaven's wants and needs. Quiet your mind so that you are receptive to My gentle voice. I call you to higher work than what the world screams for you to do. I give you a nobler calling than the world could ever offer you. Let My kingdom come to your life today.

But Jesus told him, "Follow me, and let the dead bury their own dead." Matthew 8:22

Transfer of Joy

Jesus, thank you for this time to be alone with You.
Thank you for the joy I have and I ask you for more.

YOU SEE THE snow-clad roof, brittle white clinging to black. Here in the warmth of your house - in your favorite chair - I can refill your reserves. Your level of joy has been low. You have persevered, but with no joy in your step, little gladness in your heart. You carry a façade of happiness with no real contentment in your spirit. But, there is no reason to panic, no need to despair. I replenish your joy and bring choice wine to your life. This transfer of joy takes time. It cannot be delivered in an instant. Don't rush off! Many call me Savior, but few allow Me to fully do My work in their lives. Stay longer with Me so that this transference may occur. Then, like Moses of old, you will leave this time with your heart and face changed.

Until now you have not asked for anything in my name. Ask and you will receive, and your joy will be complete. John 16:24

A Watchful State of Mind

I ask for Your guidance in all things.

WHAT YOU CONSIDER planning is often worry in disguise. There may be specific plans we make in this morning time together, but I wish for you to live in a watchful state of mind throughout the day. Spend the day looking for My presence and sensing My wishes. See this day unfold, not full of randomness and chance, but controlled by My loving and powerful hand. Your prayers have been heard, and Heaven is controlling circumstances on the kingdom's behalf. Be of good cheer because I have overcome Satan's malignant moves in this world. Go with fewer plans today. I am showing you the way to be closer to Me and how to be a more effective worker for the kingdom.

Be alert and of sober mind. Your enemy the devil prowls around like a roaring lion looking for someone to devour. 1 Peter 5:8

MARCH 2 –
As a Christian

Jesus, rework my heart and perspective so that it is in Your image. Wash away all that is not blessed by You.

USE THE PHRASE "as a Christian" more. Let it be the beginning to solving every problem, the answer to every question, the hope in every dire situation, and the starting point when you are uncertain. As a Christian, invite others. As a Christian, know that I am protecting you. As a Christian, feel the joy of My forgiveness. As a Christian, sense the power of My wisdom and guidance. As a Christian, say no to self. As a Christian, think of others first. As a Christian, do not worry. As a Christian, demonstrate patience. As a Christian, be gentle with all.

The disciples were called Christians first at Antioch.
Acts 11:26

Stay and Rest

Jesus, stay and speak with me; give me eyes to see and ears to hear You clearly.

LET THE RUSH of the earth's troubles pass you by. Quit all rushing. Stop and listen. Stay and rest. I lay much importance on your need to abide in Me. Tell Me all, but also wait for My commands to you. I often would speak into a situation you have prayed about, but you—in your fitfulness to move on—do not hear My voice. Wait for Me. I long to provide a leisurely pace for you that would do much to make you more effective for the kingdom. This is one of the benefits of knowing that you are living for eternity; it promotes a leisurely pace. Let Me speak to you in long periods of rest. Do not be a victim to the world's pace like an orphan living on the streets. You are a son and a brother.

Then, because so many people were coming and going that they did not even have a chance to eat, he said to them, "Come with me by yourselves to a quiet place and get some rest." Mark 6:31

Soul Maintenance

*Jesus, in Your kindness, do the work in my heart,
which only You can do.*

AS YOU SPEND time in My Word and with Me,
the Spirit cleans and polishes your inner being. Rich
mercy and forgiveness keep a shine on your soul. The
refreshed spirit within is evident to those who come
in contact with you. Almost imperceptibly, others can
sense the newness inside of you, the renewal of youth,
and irrepressible hope that all will be well. This time
of soul maintenance is necessary for you to have the
desired effect on the world around you. You leave these
times full of My light and with the distinct flavor that
My followers should have.

Truly my soul finds rest in God; my salvation comes
from him. Psalm 62:1

Heavenly Inspiration

Thank You for the joy of feeling useful to You.

COUNT IT YOUR richest blessing when you can help someone draw closer to Me. Move the world nearer to Me with words, actions, touch, and gentle pressure. With each opportunity to speak today, say, "Jesus, you speak first." With this simple refrain, you move your actions from self-guided to Christ-guided. Thus, you see the wisdom of heavenly inspiration over human aspiration clearly. I know the needs of each soul and what would draw them closer to Me. Sometimes I may simply ask you to be near a person so that you are the one they reach to when the storms come. My call for you to be near someone may be of more use to the kingdom than a thousand invitations.

The Spirit told Philip, "Go to that chariot and stay near it." Acts 8:29

MARCH 6 —

Belief Softens the Heart

Let me feel Your power to make all things right.

I AM THE good farmer, full of hope that heavenly seed can grow in every life and situation. All I need is fertile soil. I supply the good seed, the rain, and the sunshine. Give Me the gift of a believing heart full of hope for yourself and others. I will place you where you can sow Heaven's seed. Unbelief and doubt drive Me from the hearts of My followers and limit their kingdom use. Say to yourself in every situation, "I believe." When you stumble say, "I believe." With every utterance of faith in Me, I provide hope to your heart. I call you to sow with Me on this earth, casting gospel seeds where they might be well received. What I ask of you today is to have a faith-filled heart that allows Me to use you. A relentless pursuit of souls is still My glorious obsession. The redemption of man remains My continual work. Together we advance the kingdom. Live a life of love for others by believing you can supply what they most need—Heaven in the form of a Savior.

A farmer went out to sow his seed. Luke 8:5

The Value of Sitting Still

Show me more spiritual truths today, Lord.

LEARN FROM MY years on earth the value of sitting still. Note when I sat watching the crowd and saw the poor woman's generosity and when I sat near the well at noon and spoke with the Samaritan woman. Observe when I called the twelve to come with Me and we journeyed to the mountainside and sat down. Reflect how I, in boyhood years, sat in the temple listening and learning. Finally, rejoice that when I had finished My sacrifice on the cross, I sat down with Our Father in victory. There is a happy victory for you gained through sitting with Me, listening to the inner voice, and obeying it faithfully. Sit. Listen. Obey.

After three days they found him in the temple courts, sitting among the teachers, listening to them and asking them questions. Luke 2:46

MARCH 8 —

A Quick Look to Me

Lord, please bless the decisions I need to make today.

MEET YOUR RESPONSIBILITIES today without rush, but also without undue delay. Pray about your day when alone with Me but keep praying throughout the day. Obtain quick guidance for decisions as you consider each step. I will give you all you need. A yes or no here. A go or stop there. A quick look to Me at each turn in the day is all you need. This dependence on Me will bring you joy, calm, and success. You will find in this a godly rhythm to your day, a heavenly tempo to all you do, and a spiritual freshness in your life. This quick turning to Me will improve your decision-making and give you greater peace of mind.

When he saw Jesus passing by, he said, "Look, the Lamb of God!" John 1:36

A Full Dose of Love

Give life and joy to my day, Jesus, as only You can.

LOVE IS WHAT provides the spice to life. Life without love is mere existence. It is the intangible spiritual things that man needs the most, the greatest of these being love. Let loose of your pride and come to Me to be filled with the love you need. Let the joy that springs from My love wash away worry, bitterness, and fear. Say, "Lord, grant me a full dose of love." Take love from Me and pass it on. Love your wife, love your kids, love your friends, and love those I put on your path. Let love be in all you do and say.

Therefore if you have any encouragement from being united with Christ, if any comfort from his love, if any common sharing in the Spirit, if any tenderness and compassion, then make my joy complete by being like-minded, having the same love, being one in spirit and of one mind. Philippians 2:1–2

Be Brave

Jesus, help me to be the man I want to be.

MAN FEARS REJECTION and craves acceptance and recognition from others. This is a stumbling block for My followers who seek to put the kingdom first. When prompted by their gentle Master, they struggle to ask a friend what he may think about spiritual matters. When led by their caring Lord, they fail to invite the hurting soul He seeks to a meal. When bid by their compassionate leader to stand up for the ridiculed, they shrink back in self-preservation. Fear causes Heaven's beautiful plans to go unused. Fear causes the gift of salvation to be undelivered. But, this is not always so. Consider My servants of old and imitate their courage. There is a bravery that is connected to initiation for the kingdom. Join with My servant Paul in his willingness to be brave and considered a fool for Me. Bravery still marks the lives of My disciples.

We are fools for Christ, but you are so wise in Christ! We are weak, but you are strong! You are honored, we are dishonored! 1 Corinthians 4:10

Miracles Within

Thank you, Lord, for the miracles You perform in my heart every day.

MIRACLES EXIST AND are happening all around you. My believers marvel at the miracles of old: the providing of the plagues, the parting of the Red Sea, the raising of Lazarus, the feeding of the five thousand. However, the most important miracles to Heaven occur within the human heart. Miracles abound when the power of the cross, the overwhelming force of grace, is brought to bear on a human heart. Deadness is replaced with life. Bitterness is overcome by forgiveness. Hopelessness is exchanged for confidence. Darkness is defeated by Heaven's overpowering light. Depression is trounced by new warmth found in Me. Sin is derailed by joy found in the risen life. Satan's grasp on a soul is broken by My strong hand. Let us go together and offer to all the power of full redemption.

I will give them an undivided heart and put a new spirit in them; I will remove from them their heart of stone and give them a heart of flesh. Ezekiel 11:19

Be Content Until

Let me find satisfaction in what I do.

BE CONTENT WITH your job until I say, "Enough," and lead you to another field. You would be disobedient if I had led you to another calling, and you refused. I have rich plans for you, but My desire is for you to stay where I have placed you for now, happily discharging your duties. When I am ready, when the time is right, I will lead you to other work that you will find more meaningful. Today, faithfully complete your tasks as working for Me. Be joyful where I have placed you. For every man, difficulty in being content with his work remains as a generational curse. This is man's continual misfortune since the fall. But, rejoice! I have come to make you whole. Say to yourself today, "I am content as a son of God."

Cursed is the ground because of you; through painful toil you will eat food from it all the days of your life. It will produce thorns and thistles for you, and you will eat the plants of the field. Genesis 3:17–18

Be Comfortable

Lord, I seek Your peace.

THE AGITATION YOU feel is just below the surface but apparent to all. Be comfortable except where I call you to venture forth or change. Be comfortable with Me. Be comfortable with your wife, children, church, work, lifestyle, and current calling. To be comfortable is to be content with the life I have given you. Being comfortable is not a license for selfishness or sin, but an invitation for contentment, confidence, and peace.

But godliness with contentment is great gain.
1 Timothy 6:6

Choose Friendship

Jesus, show me the way to navigate through this stressful situation.

CAREFULLY PICK YOUR words today. Choose friendship over winning in business. Respond to no one by email regarding the situation. Let Me help swell up in you a generous spirit. You are living for eternity and the storehouses of Heaven's riches are always full. Let your confidence in your citizenship in Heaven lead you to be different than you were yesterday; a lighter touch is needed. Pride and fear block the way for a successful result.

Make every effort to live in peace with everyone and to be holy; without holiness no one will see the Lord. Hebrews 12:14

Love and Acceptance of Others

Jesus, help me be effective for You.

BE A MAN of love, and you cannot help but be effective for Me. Let that be your defining quality. This answers all the "Who am I?" questions. Make it your goal to let love sink into your inner being so that your very personality is altered. See the connection between love and acceptance of others in My life on the earth. The religious leaders demanded change before they would give their acceptance, and the result of their ministry was judgement and condemnation. The Father sent Me to save the world, not to condemn it. I loved and accepted others before they changed, before they took steps to align their lives with Heaven. Zacchaeus was thrilled to share a meal with a man who would laugh with him. The Samaritan woman felt only My love and acceptance though her sin was obvious. This is the beautiful way. Follow it. Together we go to make the orphan a son or daughter.

The Son of Man came eating and drinking, and they say, "Here is a glutton and a drunkard, a friend of tax collectors and sinners." But wisdom is proved right by her deeds. Matthew 11:19

Be Perfect

Search me, Lord, and take away all my sin.

MY INJUNCTION TO you is to be *perfect as your Father in* Heaven *is perfect.* To do this you must allow Me to point out your errors and the parts of your character that need to be refined. Here on earth you will always have struggles and will continually make mistakes. However, the Spirit of My kingdom is characterized by progress and eternal youth. Here are errors for you to avoid: listening to more than one voice, seeking reward from the world, and tackling tomorrow's burdens today. These you cannot conquer in a day or your lifetime, but together we refine the inner you, day by day, victory to victory.

Anyone who listens to the word but does not do what it says is like someone who looks at his face in a mirror and, after looking at himself, goes away and immediately forgets what he looks like. James 1:23–24

MARCH 17 –
You and I Together

Lord, I trust You with everything. Grant me inner peace as I work though today's troubles.

ONLY WHEN YOU allow Me to be truly with you do you have My peace. Increase your ability to sense My unseen presence throughout your day. Stop and rest with Me. Then, I will show you that all is well. Feel My tender closeness and affirming presence. Then, you can reflect Me to others. Share the joy and peace you have only through Me. You and I together—this is how you are to live.

When you pass through the waters, I will be with you; and through the rivers, they shall not overflow you. When you walk through the fire, you shall not be burned, nor shall the flame scorch you. Isaiah 43:2 WEB

To Be Found by Me

Lord, bless the brokenhearted.

YOU HEARD THE heartfelt prayer from the teenage boy last night: "I want to be found." This universal yearning is the curse and blessing of young and old alike. The human heart senses its separation from its heavenly home and longs to be found, longs to return. This longing rests in every man's inner being. All souls desire to be found by Me. They do not crave a religious ceremony or a church membership, but to be found by a loving Savior. Accepted. Embraced. Cared for. These yearnings draw men to Me. But, even those who have been found by Me need to be re-found every day. Re-found. Re-discovered. Re-embraced. Without the power of the cross, the soul's yearning would be a forlorn hope. But with it, all things are possible! Your friend is on his right path home.

He has made everything beautiful in its time. He has also set eternity in the human heart; yet no one can fathom what God has done from beginning to end. Ecclesiastes 3:11

Laughter and a Hearty Sense of Humor

Jesus, bring Your rest this morning as I feel unrest and trouble.

LAUGHTER SPRINGS FROM inner peace and calm. Only troubles within your heart can really harm you. Laugh and work through all earthly, temporary circumstances. Know that all is well. Believe this deep within your soul. Be assured in your secret times with Me. Too often the circles of Christian fellowship lack the mirth that should be associated with following Me. Laughter and a hearty sense of humor are a part of the heavenly atmosphere as much as holiness and reverence. Humor indicates family and acceptance, hallmarks of Heaven.

Our mouths were filled with laughter, our tongues with songs of joy. Psalm 126:2

Absolutes

Let me feel Your nearness today.

THE WORLD WARNS against speaking in absolutes. It complains that all or nothing thinking allows no room for gray. However, Heaven's values are often expressed in absolutes. At no time today, or in the future, will you be without Me. Never. You are never lost when connected with Me. You are never alone when I am by your side. You are never without useful work when I am your Master. You are never without provision for your needs. You are never lacking in protection when I am your Lord. In Me, you always have all you need.

Be strong and courageous. Do not be afraid or terrified because of them, for the LORD your God goes with you; he will never leave you nor forsake you.
Deuteronomy 31:6

Start with Yourself

Lord, be with me when I have this sense of panic.

COME TO A screeching halt! Heaven cannot work through you when you plow through your day at rapid speed. Slow down and rest. Carve out extra time today to sit with Me. Just sit with Me. Patiently wait on Me so that My peace is allowed to sink into you deeply. There is much to do, but it is the grace-filled, renewed, and replenished servant who can accomplish his Master's work. Change the world one person at a time but start with yourself. The birds have returned. The joy of spring and full supply are here.

Let the morning bring me word of your unfailing love, for I have put my trust in you. Psalm 143:8

A Wonderful Man

Thank you for Your gracious acceptance of me, even with all my faults.

IF THE OLD Testament is the story of a wayward nation, the New Testament is the story of a wonderful Man. Our loving Father sent Me to be born of woman to redeem each person to the Father's family. The world will give man labels and class distinctions of little worth. The Father sent Me to give each person the right to be adopted as His son or daughter and to become co-heirs with Me to all the Father's spiritual riches. I came to give everyone a spirt of belonging, a spirit of acceptance, and an eternal spirit of family.

Because you are his sons, God sent the Spirit of his Son into our hearts, the Spirit who calls out, "Abba, Father."
Galatians 4:6

MARCH 23 –

The Key to Contentment

Lord, help me work through my frustrations.

COMPLETE SURRENDER TO My will is the key to contentment. "What shall I do today, Lord? Where shall I go? What are You doing here, Lord?" These are the thoughts of My humble followers. The surrendered soul moves much cleaner through the day. Your agitation springs from the battles to submit your wants to Mine. Have fewer expectations other than My will be done. Trust that I know what is best for you and the kingdom. See in each interruption, each encounter, My loving plan for you. Yield to My wishes in all things, and you will gain a deep sense of peace and contentment. This rearrangement, placing My will above your own, is part of your lifelong discipleship. Daily trust the life I give you as My wonderful plan for you.

He guides the humble in what is right and teaches them his way. Psalm 25:9

The Discipline of Quiet Listening

Thank You for the blessing of Your encouragement.

YOUR STRENGTH IS that you know I am your source of power and wisdom. Help Me change this dark world by letting My light shine in. I long to speak into the life of each of My followers. The discipline of quiet listening provides a joy and effectiveness to all who practice it. Continue to wait with Me and listen for My encouragement and instructions. Go where I lead. Speak when I prompt you. Say yes when you sense a green light from Me. Say no when you sense My red light. Through your times of listening, I add a dignity to your life that cannot be acquired in any other way. I can impart to you love, joy, and peace. Changed by Me, you can affect the world.

Therefore you do not lack any spiritual gift as you eagerly wait for our Lord Jesus to be revealed to you. 1 Corinthians 1:7

Bring Me All Your Problems

Thank You for always hearing me.

AM I OVERWHELMED by your day, week, or month? Rest quietly knowing that I can handle every problem you bring to Me. My followers are to carry each other's burden, but only the world's Savior can accept the sin of man and lift his burden. Bring Me all your problems, big and small. Problems within and without. Nothing is too small or trivial to share with Me. You can never share too much with Me.

Come to me, all you who are weary and burdened, and I will give you rest. Matthew 11:28

An Invincible Life

Lord, protect me, and I will be fully protected.

IN THE BLINK of an eye, your mood can change from good to bad. Train yourself to remain calm no matter what the day may bring. You cannot control the actions of others. Even the saintliest soul sins. Learn that your inner self can always be at peace despite what happens during your day. Shielded by walls of faith, your inner being can remain calm despite the words or actions of others. There is a power to the soul that can walk through this life so shielded. Together with Me, you can lead an invincible life.

The LORD is my rock, my fortress and my deliverer; my God is my rock, in whom I take refuge, my shield and the horn of my salvation. He is my stronghold, my refuge and my savior—from violent people you save me. 2 Samuel 22:2–3

Return Here for Replenishment and Joy

Lord, my to-do list is followed by more things to do.
I feel stretched, unsalted, and full of human failings.

THIS WORLD CAN feel disruptive and even chaotic when you have tasted My inner peace. You feel stretched in a dozen directions. In part, this is merely the life stage you are in. It will not always remain so. Work, trust, and daily return here for replenishment and joy. Listen and obey. I carefully guide your steps and will not put upon you more than you can bear.

I will refresh the weary and satisfy the faint. Jeremiah 31:25

Wait until Prompted

Jesus, I know the mark I want to leave on this world, the relationships I want to have with my wife and kids, and the impact I want to have on my community. But I feel trapped at work. It is a job I no longer enjoy or in which I find satisfaction. I see Your hand working, but it appears to be working so slowly. Life and my kids seem to be passing me by.

ALWAYS WAIT UNTIL prompted by Me. Seek My blessing before you act. King Saul thought it was time to act on his own. He offered the sacrifice set aside for Samuel. Full of fear, he rushed forward. Guided by haste, he acted beyond Heaven's wishes. The timing for change is Mine. I bid you to wait and trust. I know you do not find satisfaction in your career. Fear and frustration often cause My followers to act out of step with the Spirit. Be faithful; believe I have you where you can best serve Me right now. I will not be slow to act. My timing is always perfect and My prompting clear.

And Saul offered up the burnt offering. Just as he finished making the offering, Samuel arrived, and Saul went out to greet him. "What have you done?" asked Samuel. 1 Samuel 13:9–11

Make Heaven Real

Jesus, You are light and life. Thank You for Your gospel of grace.

HOW CAN MY gospel make a difference in the world today? Partner with Heaven to make it relevant to a restless generation. Even in a life full of ruin, there is beauty and value. Love the good you see in all. This was My way of making the gospel relevant to those I met while on the earth. The Samaritan woman felt loved by Me before she changed. Zacchaeus sensed acceptance before he followed Me. To be a man who sees the good in others is to arm yourself with Heaven's weapons. There is good in all; your task is to see it even if the person you are helping does not see it themselves. Tell others, "I see this in you." I will help you to see the good in others and then give you the courage to tell them. And so, you make Heaven real for those around you.

So God created mankind in his own image, in the image of God he created them; male and female he created them. Genesis 1:27

MARCH 30 —
Quiet Repose

Lord, refresh me in this important time I spend with You.

LET ME HELP you find a balance between conversation and quiet repose. Too many words from you drown out your awareness of My presence and My voice. Your task is to open corners of the earth to My influence. If you live outside My presence, you are not available to provide the love, help, and encouragement I seek to interject in the world around you. Again, you are not to do all things, but only those things I place on your heart. Come back with Me into quiet repose. Do this to help those around you.

Very well then, with foreign lips and strange tongues God will speak to this people, to whom he said, "This is the resting place, let the weary rest"; and "This is the place of repose"—but they would not listen. Isaiah 28:11–12

Bless Ever More

I love You for the assurance You give me over my fears.
I love You for the guidance that makes me feel useful.
I love You for being gentle and not harsh. Being with
You is the best part of my day.

THIS MORNING SWING wide the door to your heart. Allow Me to bless you ever more. To know Me is to have love, joy, and peace. To have Me in your life is to gain wholeness. The world rages on with a restless pace. I stand at the door of each heart and knock—the gentle Christ searching for souls to save and bless. All work you do for Me is miracle work if your guided steps allow My true gifts to pass from Me to others.

Save your people and bless your inheritance; be their shepherd and carry them forever. Psalm 28:9

Be Transformed

Lord, thank You for this vacation, my family, sunshine, warmer temperatures, and plentiful food and drink. Thank You for all my circumstances, because I know You use them to lead me closer to You. Help me to lean not on my own understanding, but trust You completely.

ALL TIME IS golden when lived in My presence. Is there a greater gift—a more precious one—than awareness of My presence? Ask for this today, and it will be granted to you. Leave business and work worries behind you. Let Me handle all of those. Soak in a rich sense of My presence, and you cannot help but be transformed into My likeness. Be soft and positive in all your conversations, mild and mellow in your spirit, and warm and giving in your nature. Bow your head and let Me bless you.

And we all, who with unveiled faces contemplate the Lord's glory, are being transformed into his image with ever increasing glory, which comes from the Lord. 2 Corinthians 3:18

Coat Yourself with My Gentleness

Lord, cleanse my heart of bitterness, anger, and criticalness. Rid me of these spirits. Instill in me Your positive flow of joy, peace, and the childlike spirit that is friendly to all and sees the best in everyone.

SATAN IS THE thief who seeks to rob and steal. He takes joy, self-worth, and innocence. He has lost, but that does not mean he does not try and try again. His effect on the world—the effect of sin—is to make it cold with harsh edges. His desire is to make the world, and all the souls in the world, downcast and full of despair. But, he loses as sure as winter loses to spring. The end of his story is defeat. Coat yourself with My gentleness; it flows from trust in My power to right all evil, both within and without. Gentleness has been lacking in your character. Imitate Me. I am gentle and meek.

Let your gentleness be evident to all. The Lord is near. Philippians 4:5

APRIL 3 —
Love and Hope

Lord, show me Your path.

LOVE CAN CHANGE every environment and be applied in every circumstance. Love those you are with. Love those you meet. Christian love spread all around elevates an earthly atmosphere to a heavenly one. If life seems plain, My love element is missing. Hope is always yours in Me. This makes you invincible. What can really harm you? Nothing can touch your hope of Heaven. Hope is also your belief that I am working for you in all things here and now as you move toward the Heaven that awaits you.

May your unfailing love be with us, LORD, even as we put our hope in you. Psalm 33:22

The Secret Ingredient

Thank You for the beauty I see in Your creation all around me.

GOLDFISH SWIMMING in their pond. Birds aloft in their tree. Boats afloat on their river. Man upright with his God. All is right in the world. Walk upright with Me today. No slouching. Stand tall, as tall as you can, and wait for My good plans to unfold. You and your family are not orphans cast aside and subject to the capricious pangs of this world. No! That is another voice you hear. Today is My day like all other days. I know your name, your needs and wants, your cares and worries. I know you well, indeed, better than you know yourself. Crock-pot meals are slow-cooked. A microwaved plan is not for you. I have something better—much better. It all begins with your will. Once that is placed in My hands, I can arrange, plan, and move Heaven and earth for you. Your task is to want only My will for your life. Throw away all else. Say to yourself, "May Your will be done." The surrender of your will to Me is the secret ingredient I need to do My work in and through you.

For I have come down from heaven not to do my own will but the will of him who sent me. John 6:38

The Father Still Works

Lord, grant me the good work that only comes from Heaven.

OUR FATHER STILL works in the world today in season and out of season. Open spiritual eyes so you can see. Good from Heaven above is present all around you. Evil is present in this world too, but it is limited in power and duration. Be a useful worker today, a true member of Your Father's family. He is the God of today. He desires everyone to be saved. Be a man who desires to be in the spiritual battle with Me.

In his defense Jesus said to them, "My Father is always at his work to this very day, and I too am working." John 5:17

APRIL 6 –
Healing Touch

Lord, in Your mercy, fix me this morning.

I LAY MY hand on you in blessing. My touch is as powerful now as it was two thousand years ago. One touch from Me, one interaction, and all that ails you can be healed. Wait in love and confidence to feel My touch. As you wait, courage and hope will flow into your being, irradiating your life with the warmth of My presence. Trust replaces fear. Belief removes doubt. Hope is substituted for exasperation. Spiritual healing was why I came to the earth and why I still come.

And the people all tried to touch Him, because power was coming from him and healing them all. Luke 6:19

APRIL 7 –

Your Privacy

Lord, I surrender my irritability and worry to Your mighty hand. I strive for joy and contentment, but fall short daily. You know the help I need.

PRIVACY IS A basic human need. Here with Me you have your privacy—our time alone where no one can see you or where you are going. Here no one can disturb you, and you are free from other's interruptions. Alone you sit on Heaven's stairway in My perfect light. Here we speak as friends. You can share all with Me because I know you better than you know yourself. There is no condemnation with Me. From here you can arise rested with a feeling of being fully understood and with new insights into your problems.

You are my hiding place; you will protect me from trouble and surround me with songs of deliverance. Psalm 32:7

APRIL 8 –

Holy Is Our Father

Lord, show me the Father.

HOLY IS OUR Father and all that surrounds His throne room. There is no pretension there. He is perfect, loving, kind, and just. He is all-powerful, all-knowing, and worthy of your honor and worship. I am all that My Father is as well—seasoned with My stint in human form. Together We plan for you and bless you. We watch over your family and supply all your needs. You have an invisible bubble of protection and care around you. Serve Me out of the strength and joy that this knowledge provides for you.

Day and night they never stopped saying, "Holy, holy, holy is the Lord God Almighty," who was, and is, and is to come. Revelation 4:8

Love in Abundance

Lord, You are the Vine I need. In faith, I abide in You and believe You will supply all I need, including work inspired by joy.

LOVE IS THE world's greatest resource. In Me you have love in abundance. This is why Christianity outshines other philosophies. Say today, "I accept Your abundant love for me and give it to others." The power source is Me, and I am yours in full measure. Give when you feel prompted. Speak when you are urged. Act when you feel you ought.

Mercy, peace and love be yours in abundance. Jude 1:2

The Way to Overcome

*Lord, show me how to live without fear or show me the
way to overcome it.*

WITH EVERY OBSTACLE, remember who is able to
keep you from falling. Daily put your trust in Me, and
I will show you the way to overcome. Believe when
you cannot see. Trust when you do not feel like trusting. Hope when hope escapes you. Love when you feel
rejected. Rejoice when you are low. Open your heart
wide, and I will come to you and help you overcome
whatever obstacle may be in your life. Remember, there
can be no failure when you are with Me.

Who is it that overcomes the world? Only the one who
believes that Jesus is the Son of God. 1 John 5:5

APRIL 11 –
Move On

Lord, help me to understand this business failing and the depressing spirit that it brings to me.

I WILL NOT forget you. Gladly accept My will for you. Some paths come to a dead-end, not a fork in the road. However, a dead-end does not mean a mistaken path. My path for you is not always linear. Say, "Not my will, but His. Not my choice, but His." I will complete unfinished work and mend what is broken. Move on and accept the new blessings I have for you.

Brother and sisters, I do not consider myself yet to have taken hold of it. But, one thing I do: Forgetting what is behind and straining toward what is ahead, I press on toward what is ahead, I press on toward the goal to win the prize for which God has called me heavenward in Christ Jesus. Philippians 3:13–14

Your Own Personal Resurrection

Lord, thank You for this Easter celebration and the power of Your resurrection.

I CAME TO save the whole world. Your own life was broken in pieces and strewn asunder. My mercy came to you and made you complete and whole. I came to save all the world, but I want you to have a strong sense of your own personal resurrection in Me. Say, "I believe in the power of His resurrection in me."

We were therefore buried with him through baptism into death in order that, just as Christ was raised from the dead through the glory of the Father, we too may live a new life. Romans 6:4

The One Who Overcomes

Lord, help me to trust You completely. I claim Your help. Be near to me today.

YOU SEEK ME, and so you will find Me, today as every day. Despite your shortcomings and giving-ins, you are My perfect follower, made right by love and grace. So often I long to rush in and take away your burdens—financial and emotional—but what would that gain you? The current circumstances are instilling the mettle I need in you. Moment to moment, day by day, keep believing, trusting, and praying. It is dawn, and the light has come. I bless the one who overcomes.

To him who overcomes, I will give to eat from the tree of life which is in the midst of the Paradise of God. Revelation 2:7 NKJV

The Hardworking Holy Spirit

Allow me to sense Your presence and hear just a little of Your will.

ALIGN YOUR WILL with My will. Joy will be the result, the joy that springs from heavenly purpose. My will is made known to you through the hardworking Holy Spirit, who yearns to find ready vessels on the earth to do kingdom work. Say to yourself, "My life is not my own, but God's to use and direct." This mindset changes you, gives you a humble heart, and readies you for use. Many missions await—fulfilling God adventures. Let the Holy Spirit find you available today and every day.

All that belongs to the Father is mine. That is why I said the Spirit will receive from me what he will make known to you. John 16:15

Live Gratefully Today

Jesus, help me this morning with all the thoughts that come rushing toward me.

GOD DESIGNED MAN to live one day at a time with little need to plan for the future. Man has turned this principle on its head; worry, fret, and fear flood in from tomorrow. I know your needs. I know your struggles, and I am your great deliverer. My command for you is to live gratefully with Me today. Look for reasons to smile. Then, I will be there and will be found by you. Do no planning today. Your simple task is to look for reasons to smile. Fill the day with glad turnings to Me and simple thank-yous.

Give thanks in all circumstances; for this is God's will for you in Christ Jesus. 1 Thessalonians 5:18

Renewal of Mind, Body, and Soul

Thank You for help when I feel like my life is falling apart.

WHEN YOUR PART of the earth draws closer to the sun, when the air warms and the birds come north again, spring breaks forth on the earth like the first time. I specialize in *new*, in fresh starts and happy beginnings. My creation includes recreating and the renewal of mind, body, and soul of those who are Mine. Your life is not falling apart; I, your personal Creator, renew and replenish your heart.

That person is like a tree planted by streams of water, which yields its fruit in season and whose leaf does not wither—whatever they do prospers. Psalm 1:3

The Hopeful Turning

Jesus, thank You for the beauty I see all around me.

LET NATURE'S JOYOUS new beginning cause springtime in your heart on this perfect morning. Spiritual and physical renewal are yours, as always, when you turn to Me. And that—the hopeful turning—consistently done, day after day, is your greatest strength. It is why you have consistent hope, first for yourself and then for others. I give you hope for your scarred and broken life, and you are able to help others who are scarred and broken. This is My plan. Place your hope in Me. All is well, even when you do not see it. Let your hope in the deep and rich plan I have for you give you encouragement. I will reveal it step by step as is appropriate. Say today, "I have hope in Jesus for myself and for others."

May the God of hope fill you with all joy and peace as you trust in him, so that you may overflow with hope by the power of the Holy Spirit. Romans 15:13

APRIL 18 –

Cheerful Christianity

Guide us as we look for a church home.

GUARD AGAINST FALSE doctrine but let go of human hang-ups masquerading as convictions. I desire freedom. Embrace the spiritual and mental health that comes from freedom. Accept the cheerful Christianity of a soul dedicated to Me in love. Let go of rules, stipulations, and regulations that are not based on My Word. Cheerful Christianity is not cheap Christianity; I came to save man, not condemn him. I came to provide love and laughter, not heartache and pettiness. The religion I founded was to be rooted in joy and good news. How can the religion based on free grace be anything but joyful? Man has soured its message with a focus on rules and his own performance. Grace and love are my weapons against evil forces. Embrace grace. Embrace love. Say no to the negative and critical thoughts from the evil one. Instead, hear My voice saying, "I love you and am proud of you."

These rules, which have to do with things that are all destined to perish with use, are based on merely human commands and teachings. Colossians 2:22

A Lighter Approach

Thank You, Jesus, for Your love for me and all of mankind. Let me live in that love and be Your friend and help change this world.

MY GOSPEL IN a word is *love*, but there is nothing in you that creates love. So how can you give it to others unless you receive it from Me? Sit here with Me for a longer period. My love and thought for you can permeate your whole being and inspire and illuminate all you do and say. It is an unalterable law that no man can be with Me and remain unchanged. Pray more. Talk to Me more. Absorb My life, love, and approach. Love and laughter are often the keys to opening the door to another's heart. Remove the seriousness from your approach knowing that only I can change people. Relax and breathe deeper with the conviction that it is your Lord who makes the opportunities and pulls others to Him. A lighter approach is a more effective way.

For we are God's handiwork, created in Christ Jesus to do good works, which God prepared in advance for us to do. Ephesians 2:10

Love's Gentle Pressure

Lord, help me to listen and obey all that You desire for me today.

THE KINGDOM OFTEN advances through love's gentle pressure. That is how I speak to you throughout the day. Improve your sensitivity to the Spirit's promptings. The world shouts at you. The pleasures, worries, and day-to-day business of this life crowd out Heaven's commands. To aid the hearing of My voice say, "May Your kingdom be first." This signals to Heaven that you desire to serve Me and advance the kingdom. Do this and your heart will sense love's gentle pressure.

Seek first his kingdom and his righteousness, and all these things will be given to you as well. Matthew 6:33

I Am a Son of God

Orchestrate my life, Lord. Help me strain out all that hinders the risen life.

COME TO ME for direction, peace, and security. Stay here long enough to receive My blessing. Do not venture out until you feel blessed: blessed by the Father, blessed by Me, and comforted by the Holy Spirit. Say, "I am a son of God." Say this as a reminder of your true identity, which is hidden in Heaven. Say it as a shout of praise to the God who loves you. Say it to remove evil. Say it as a reminder that the gift of joyous kingdom work is yours. All is light and good here.

"I will be a Father to you, and you will be my sons and daughters," says the Lord Almighty. 2 Corinthians 6:18

The Spirit Moves!

*You move the clouds as You please. Move in my life
with my consent and gratitude.*

A BIRD MAY glide. A horse may gallop. A man may
run. But the Spirit moves! Go into today calmly led by
My Spirit. Silently, but powerfully, He moves in your
life. He moves every day and at all times of the day.
Make it your goal to be more Spirit-sensitive. Follow
His gentle promptings for the spiritual success that advances My kingdom: a word of encouragement here,
the ability to remain silent there, a cheerful countenance to all.

Since we live by the Spirit, let us keep in step with the
Spirit. Galatians 5:25

Live in a Spirit of Appreciation

Lord Jesus, help me today to control my mind and give me a spirit of contentment.

WHEN TIRED NATURE pushes you out of spiritual peace, I stand by your side, protecting you from the enemy's darts, arrows, and stings. When you are pressed and pinned down, I come to rescue you. I come to return you to the freshness that is from above. Only love can recreate and restore. Expect less today and appreciate more. Appreciate every hour you have been given. There is much to be thankful for. Live more in a spirit of appreciation for what you have been given and less in comparing yourself to others. Appreciate the work I am doing in you and through you.

I have learned the secret of being content in any and every situation, whether well fed or hungry, whether living in plenty or want. Philippians 4:12

A Beautiful Life to Shine Forth

Thank you, Father God and Lord Jesus, for Your encouraging presence. Change me from the inside and take away all my sin.

A FLOWER. A bird. A sunset. All these are created by Me. Beauty is part of Heaven's core. It is a beautiful life Our Father intends each of His children to have. There can be a beauty to human life here on earth even when it lacks perfection. A flower with an imperfection still displays splendor. A real life, full of inadequacies, can be a beautiful life—restored each day by Heaven's love and kindness. Come back to My grace and acceptance. Daily I rebuild and reshape your inner being; I clean and polish your soul when it is marred by sin. I enable a beautiful life to shine forth.

For God, who said, "Let light shine out of darkness," made his light shine in our hearts to give us the light of the knowledge of God's glory displayed in the face of Christ. 2 Corinthians 4:6

My Book of Remembrance

Help me, Lord. I am fretful and downcast. Restore me and give me hope.

I COME IN grace and truth. Satan longs to operate like a black box for your life. He seeks to record and keep your errors and mistakes. He is quick to point out your failures and what caused them. He desires to show you, again and again, what has gone wrong in your life. My book of remembrance for your life is covered by My forgiveness. I seek to remind you of all you have done right and the times when you have aligned yourself with Heaven's royal guard. Fix your eyes on Me, and your life will be full of grace to yourself and others. No harsh judgements are allowed here.

Then those who feared the LORD spoke to one another, and the LORD gave attention and heard it, and a book of remembrance was written before Him for those who fear the LORD and who esteem His name. Malachi 3:16 NASB

Be Ambitious for the Kingdom of Heaven

I believe You can use me. Put me where I can do the most good.

AMBITION IS GOOD when I am leading. Ambition is wholesome when others benefit. Have the audacity to embrace Heaven's acceptance of you. It is what every man needs but is too ashamed to admit. Receive it and be ready to pass heavenly secrets along to others. I need My followers to be ambitious for the kingdom. Know in your heart that there are souls who only you can reach for Me. Preoccupation with self hinders many Christians from being effective for Me. Do not think of yourself at all; only know that I can transform any person I put on your path. Be confident that you can help a lost soul turn to Me because you know the power of your Savior. I can change all but need My workers to introduce Me to a lost and hurting world. Be ambitious for the kingdom of Heaven.

It has always been my ambition to preach the gospel where Christ was not known, so that I would not be building on someone else's foundation. Romans 15:20

My Unconditional Love

Jesus, protect me from my mistakes.

YOUR FAITH IS like a walled city, a fortress protecting you. You may be besieged, but your life is well-guarded. Arrows of shame, guilt, and fear are shot over your walls, but here with Me you feel no reproach. Your walled city is built stone by stone, one faithful thought upon another faithful thought. Today, say, "My Lord loves me no matter what." Let that victory chant allow you to push back the fears of the day and the accusations that come to your mind. Let your faith in My unconditional love signal the devil's defeat.

David then took up residence in the fortress, and so it was called the City of David. 1 Chronicles 11:7

I Am Your Great Friend

Jesus, thank You for spending this time with me.

MOVE PAST ELEMENTARY teachings about Me. Share with others that it is not knowing about Me that changes you; it is knowing Me. You know Me, and you have the joy of belonging to Heaven's family. Here with Me you have My divine companionship. You have the good feeling of being linked with a warm, gentle, and loving God, a God who is not self-seeking, but desires to see all His children content and cared for. Can anything be more life-changing than friendship with the Son of Man? I am your great Friend.

Therefore, let us move beyond the elementary teachings about Christ and be taken forward to maturity, not laying again the foundation of repentance from acts that lead to death, and of faith in God. Hebrews 6:1

Smiles instead of Stares

As I say Your name, Jesus, grant me all that You have promised.

JOYFULLY YOU SHOULD adore Me. Have a softer heart today and a warmer personality. Let trust replace fear. Approach others with smiles instead of stares. Let My hope fill you in lieu of despair. Become ever younger and more cheerful as you grow older. I will always have meaningful, inspiring work for you. A softer heart and warmer countenance are signs of your Christian progress.

A happy heart makes the face cheerful, but heartache crushes the spirit. Proverbs 15:13

Your Family Legacy

Jesus, show me all the steps You would have me take today.

BLAZE A TRAIL that others can follow. Your legacy will not be as a titan of industry. You will not be known for discoveries in a lab, exploits in a sport, or fine closing arguments in a courtroom. No, your legacy is one born of humility and the simple belief that a loving God came back to earth to help every person make it back home. Your testimony is that the broken can be healed, the lost can be found, and the impure can be made pure again. Your testimony is that grace and love can build a family, and the God who spoke still speaks. Your family legacy is born of a simple faith and a return to Christian roots.

We will not hide them from their descendants; we will tell the next generation the praiseworthy deeds of the LORD, his power, and the wonders he has done. Psalm 78:4

MAY 1 –

Each Day a Blank Canvas

Show me Your good and pleasing will.

MANY OF THE pursuits you have preplanned are shallow. Deny yourself and let Me have My way. Rest with Me this morning, and I will not only show you My way; I will live this day with you. All I need is your request. Say, "Come with me, Jesus. Stay with me." View each day as a blank canvas, new and unused, without a mark on it—a clean surface, ready for the Master's hand. Let Me pick the subject and the colors. Let Heaven's hues color your life and work. See Me be in all the details throughout the day.

Then he said to them all: "Whoever wants to be my disciple must deny themselves and take up their cross daily and follow me." Luke 9:23

Joyful Hours

Lord, forgive me for not spending the time with You that I should.

WHEN YOUR DAY is rushed, when you have little or no abiding with Me, then your day presses upon you with heaviness, with a lack of joy. Here with Me, imperceptibly, you receive peace and sustenance for your soul. Stay long enough so that you arc spiritually full. Glad days result when My peace rests within you. Joyful hours spring from awareness of My presence. Say, "Jesus is here with me."

The fruit of the Spirit is love, joy, peace, forbearance, kindness, goodness, faithfulness, gentleness, and self-control. Against such things there is no law. Galatians 5:22–23

Spiritual Refreshment

Jesus, let me feel useful to You.

I MAKE THE opportunities for you, but at times you are not ready to take on My tasks. This may be no fault of your own; you may be depleted spiritually, emotionally, or physically. The remedy is a time of refreshment. Give yourself a fresh start by clothing yourself with My grace and rejuvenation. I will provide you with secure plans and bright hopes for useful work. Let your spiritual batteries be recharged; then kingdom work will follow. It will follow.

He refreshes my soul. He guides me along the right paths for his name's sake. Psalm 23:3

MAY 4 –

Your Discipleship

Let me be a first-class disciple of You, Jesus.

YOUR DISCIPLESHIP IS to submit every area of your life to Me, your great friend and Master. It is then you can be led by My Spirit in all things. It is submission to My written Word and also submission to the little injunctions I give you. It is the giving up of the ignoble for the noble and the commonplace for the glorious. This is your lifework on this earth as you focus on one area of your life and then another. It continues as you reach one life stage and then the next. It is work inspired by your love for Me. It is the building of a beautiful life dedicated in love to your Savior, who loves you more than you can fathom.

In the same way, those of you who do not give up everything you have cannot be my disciples. Luke 14:33

The Power of the Invitation

I want You front and center in my day, Lord.

I WANT TO be the traveling companion of all My followers, but Heaven's respect for man's free will often leaves even My followers unaware of My nearness to them. I wait. I wait for the invitation to live life with them. Oh, the power of the invitation! Invite Me to come along with you, and I am your true companion, turning dreary to meaningful, dark to light, and despair to joy. Invite Me to walk with you. I would not have continued with My followers on the Emmaus Road if not for their invitation.

They urged him strongly, "Stay with us, for it is nearly evening; the day is almost over." So he went in to stay with them. Luke 24:29

I Am the Master Planner

Lord, help me to submit to Your will when things do not go as I had hoped.

YOU WILL SEE that even in this life I am the Master Planner who gives great attention to detail. Trust Me in all that I ask you to do. Allow Me to call you to make sacrifices here and there. Take comfort when you deny yourself for My wants, knowing that I plan well for you. When I bid you to give up something that you love, push away your feelings of disappointment. Trust fully that I have prepared something much better. What I envision happening in your future is far greater than what you can imagine.

"My food," said Jesus, "is to do the will of him who sent me and to finish his work." John 4:34

148 | Heaven Calling

My Power Calms Your Soul

Jesus, help provide solutions to the problems I face today.

I KNOW YOUR frets and worries. The solution to your problems is to focus less on them and more on Me. Let your acknowledgement of My power calm your soul. The Lord who created the world is big enough to provide solutions to all the problems you face. Your difficulty is not that your problems are too large, but your view of My power is too small. Let the Holy Spirit help you to comprehend the strength of Heaven. You will see that when you view your frets and worries after this realization, they will melt away into valley irritants. It is then, once righted with Me, that I will provide the guidance you need.

But, I will sing of your power; Yes, I will sing aloud of Your mercy in the morning; For You have been my defense and refuge in the day of my trouble.
Psalm 59:16 NKJV

I Will Make Up the Difference

Lord, let me begin with You today when my spirit is downcast.

DERBY DAY IS a two-minute run for the roses. Run for My kingdom. You are stretched right now. However, you and your family are safe in My keeping. This is not a pointless race for you. I am building character in you that will benefit My kingdom. I am providing experiences in your life that will help you serve others. Trust Me with all the details of your life. When you feel that you have lost spiritual and material blessings, know that I will make up the difference even in this life.

For in him you have been enriched in every way—with all kinds of speech and with all knowledge—God thus confirming our testimony about Christ among you.
1 Corinthians 1:5–6

Joyous Work

Let me know the joy of serving You.

YOU HAVE OTHER joyous work to do that I have not yet made known to you. I reveal your work for Me daily because My followers must live day to day. There is danger in telling before the right time. But you have seen glimmers of your life to come, and it brings you hope. Work—much work—remains. I will show you clearly your kingdom work. My followers are to be simple people, taking their manna from Me each day. It is enough that I am with you this day.

Then the Lord said to Moses, "I will rain down bread from heaven for you. The people are to go out each day and gather enough for that day." Exodus 16:4

My Calm, Quiet, and Rest

Lord, provide me with all that I lack.

WHEN YOU LIVE your life going one hundred miles an hour, you cannot see the beauty all around you. Today, take on My calm, quiet, and rest. Imitate My life as found in the Scriptures. Understand that there was no rush in My words or actions. See My discipline to pull back and rest. Worry and uncertainty drive the pace you have been setting. It does not reflect a man who trusts Me with all his heart. Obey the things I lay on your heart to do and speak to Me about your worries and concerns. I will provide you with My calm, quiet, and rest.

This is what the Sovereign LORD, the Holy One of Israel says: "In repentance and rest is your salvation, in quietness and trust is your strength, but you would have none of it." Isaiah 30:15

Positive Peer Pressure

Lord, thank You for giving me the girl of my dreams.
Watch over our marriage and protect us.

LET MY GENTLE hand guide you and your wife. You often do not see the progress being made. I must bring you and your wife along together as you lean on each other for encouragement. You have the blessing of being with a Christian spouse who is like-minded in all things spiritual. You provide each other positive peer pressure to fulfill the calling from Heaven to live for Me and the kingdom. Each year grow kinder and more tender with each other. Build her up. Be her biggest fan.

He who finds a wife finds what is good and receives favor from the LORD. Proverbs 18:22

Touched by Jesus

Jesus, thank You for Your nearness to me.

"**TOUCHED BY GOD**" is a phrase that might be used to describe a talented musician or artist. It indicates that a gift has been bestowed on them, giving them the ability to do something beyond the ordinary, to provide others with something beautiful. To walk with Me daily is to allow your life to be touched by God. My touch brings healing and joy, peace, and supply. As your heart overflows with this joy, you can provide light, grace, and hope to others. A life touched by Me is a life of conquest and influence. Say today, "My life has been touched by Jesus."

Jesus reached out his hand and touched the man. "I am willing," he said, "Be clean!" Immediately he was cleansed of his leprosy. Matthew 8:3

Love in Abundance

Lord, thank You for the acceptance I feel here with You.

LOVE IS THE most valuable commodity in the world. Man's need is to be reunited with Heaven and to be loved deeply. If only every soul in the world knew what it needed. No amount of money, career success, athletic achievement, or academic accomplishment can satisfy the soul's need. No pleasure from sin can gratify it. No earthly relationship can fulfill it. Heaven waits with open arms for each person to turn to it. Love is yours in abundance. You have in Me an inexhaustible supply of love for all your needs.

The grace of our Lord was poured out on me abundantly, along with the faith and love that are in Christ Jesus. 1 Timothy 1:14

MAY 14 –
Your Path to Victory

I feel stuck today, Lord. Show me the way.

THERE IS STILL a place you can go for peace. You can always go home in your heart: a place of quiet and rest with cool shade and a light breeze. With soft footfall, I approach and sit with you. Stay here. Block out all that pulls you away from this quiet abode. Abide with Me. Peter, James, and John sought a physical kingdom from Me, a nation with borders. You make the same error now when you seek to repair the outward circumstances in your life. My kingdom is within you, and your path to victory is found inside you. Your answers are spiritual, not physical. When you are righted with Me, the external pressures are eliminated.

Nor will people say, "Here it is," or "There it is," because the kingdom of God is within you. Luke 17:21.

The Next Thing

Jesus, allow me to feel the joy of being useful to You.

BEES POLLINATE FLOWER to flower. Their Lord guides them. Christians move task to task. Their Master determines their steps. During your day when you feel useless, turn to Me and ask, "Lord, what is the next thing?" Let that prayer indicate your readiness to be used by Me. There is much to do, and our partnership brings heavenly rewards. These pauses are invitations for Me to plant in you those things, big and small, that serve the kingdom. Be ready to hear My requests, and be quick to obey. Joyous work awaits through which you will be richly rewarded.

Walk in obedience to all that the Lord your God has commanded you, so that you may live and prosper and prolong your days in the land that you will possess. Deuteronomy 5:33

During Your Waiting Time

May Your will be done, and if that will is to wait and trust, praise Your name and grant me Your peace.

ANYONE CAN FEEL safe and secure when all is going well. I call you to a higher level of faith in Me. I call you to be of good cheer when all is not going well in temporal matters. When the answers you seek seem far away, come to Me for the peace that passes understanding. I call you to strengthen your belief in Me during your waiting time. Know without a doubt that I am your kind Savior who longs to rush in and save. Tell Me you are convinced that I long to save you, and that I am fully empowered to deliver you. Believe that you are dear to Me even before you see My deliverance.

Wait for the LORD; be strong and take courage and wait for the LORD. Psalm 27:14

Love Will Open the Right Doors

Lord, lead me according to Your good and pleasing will. I love You and trust Your leadership. Show me how I can do a beautiful thing for You.

LOVE IS SIMPLE and candid, without pretense, and overwhelmingly strong. Love will open the right doors. Love will show you where you can serve Me best. Yes, serve your church, but service for Me should be so much more. My followers should not rely on those serving Me in the church to be the sole source of their ministry direction. This produces sameness and staleness—work that lacks My creativity. I came to be intimate with each of My followers. Let Me, let love, show you where and how you can serve Me.

Then I heard the voice of the Lord saying, "Whom shall I send? And who will go for us?" And I said, "Here am I. Send me!" Isaiah 6:8

A Life Full of Purpose and Joy

Master, give me the gift of a renewed spirit and heart.
In Your great mercy, pull me closer to You.

LET ME SET you free, and you will be free indeed. My power and purposes defeat the generational patterns you fight against. I wish to lead you to a life full of purpose and joy. I seek to remove the doldrums and melancholy from your life. Living with purpose defeats the empty feeling man is often left with at the end of a day. I long to give you a life full of meaning and joy. Say to yourself this day, "Jesus, I claim Your plan for my life. I claim Your cheerfulness."

"For I know the plans I have for you," declares the LORD, "plans to prosper you and not to harm you, plans to give you hope and a future." Jeremiah 29:11

Heaven's Peace and Tranquility

Lord, I pray for Your encouragement. Pierce this spiritual fog that seems so dense all around me.

TIME PASSES AND despair creeps back into your mind. You hear the ticktock from the clock on the wall, and you sense that time is passing you by. Your anxiety creeps back in. Be transformed by the eternal life that has been given to you. Eternity is difficult for man to grasp, but picture it pouring from Heaven in immensity, full of Our Father's peace and tranquility. Fog lasts only until the blazing sun burns it away. Let the eternal life in you replace despair with Heaven's peace and tranquility.

I write these things to you who believe in the name of the Son of God so that you may know that you have eternal life. 1 John 5:13

Have Love and You Have All

Thank You for the beauty of this sunrise.

LOVE IS LIKE the sun breaking through the dark horizon at daybreak. It is an irresistible force that is all-conquering. Darkness shrinks back, defeated. Love is simple and candid; it is without pretense and always builds up. Love will open the right doors as you come to them. Love is the key ingredient for any work for Me. Love warms the hearts of others. Love softens the blows of failure. Love puts the grin back on your face when frustrations press. It never loses and never backs down. If you have My love in abundance, you cannot help but succeed. The best laid plans are worthless without it, the best sermon pointless if not spurred by it, the family lost that does not contain it, and the workplace a drudgery if it is absent. Have love, and you have all.

And now these three remain: faith, hope, and love. But the greatest of these is love. 1 Corinthians 13:13

The Spiritual Lottery

Jesus, I trust You and look to You for material supply.

YOUR VIEW OF finances can reach the level of idolatry. Your goals can become obsessions. Your security is in Me, not in the decrease or increase of your debt. Do not let a financial crisis cause a spiritual and mental crisis. Instead, refocus on the spiritual lottery you have won with Me. You have won full measure of forgiveness, eternal life, love, joy, peace, and a guided life. See a lesson from My disciples who fretted about a lack of material supply when I wished them to focus on the spiritual. I alone am your strong foundation. Push back worry and obsession from your mind. Say to yourself, "Jesus is my mighty fortress. Nothing can harm me."

Aware of their discussion, Jesus asked, "You of little faith, why are you talking among yourselves about having no bread?" Matthew 16:8

Discipline Your Mind

Lord, I want to be different. I want to be changed.

YOUR FAITH IS like a flashlight cutting through a dense fog. The stronger its light, the clearer your path. Wonderful are My plans for you. You have a heart that trusts Me as your loving Savior, but you have a mind riddled with doubt and worry. Build a reserve of calm trust with Me in your heart here in the morning and then discipline your mind to stay faithful. Say to yourself, "I trust the power of Jesus."

For God has not given us a spirit of timidity, but of power and love and discipline. 2 Timothy 1:7 NASB

Be Faithful in the Small Things

Lord, let me have a life that is worthwhile; help me to do worthwhile things.

BE FAITHFUL IN the small things. Man seeks to be the architect of his life. Let Me design your life. I have wonderful plans. Follow My little injunctions, My simple requests, and do My quiet errands. Be faithful in the small things, and you will be a kingdom hero. What the world views as ordinary, may be extraordinary from Heaven's point of view. With your small acts of service for the kingdom, you build the life I have designed for you.

Whoever can be trusted with very little can also be trusted with much, and whoever is dishonest with very little will also be dishonest with much. Luke 16:10

Heaven Can Be Wherever You Let It In

Lord, be with me (I invite You in). Cleanse me, make me whole, and send me out to serve You.

HEAVEN CAN BE wherever you let it in. Let My love for you awaken your love for others. As your heart comes to life here with Me, seek ways to share with others how I perform a miracle in your heart each day without fail. Can man have a greater gift than to know the source of his true peace and happiness? You know the secret to revival. You know how to tap into unlimited encouragement and hope. Do not hide your light under a bushel. In humility share, "I'm a mess too, but He fixes me every day."

In the same way, let your light shine before others, that they may see your good deeds and glorify your Father in heaven. Matthew 5:16

Jesus Is with Me

Jesus, help me to be close to You all the time.

FACE TODAY WITH Me. Let My presence smooth the rough edges of your personality. Live life with Me, minute by minute, hour by hour. Picture Me beside you as you would a close friend. Say to yourself, "Jesus is with Me." When joy has escaped you, "Jesus is with Me." In the face of temptation, "Jesus is with Me." When fears assail, "Jesus is with Me." When life is dull, "Jesus is with me."

Instead, clothe yourself with the presence of the Lord Jesus Christ. And don't let yourself think about ways to indulge your evil desires. Romans 13:14 NLT

The Joy of Belonging

May Your path for us be clear. Help us to find the right church home.

WHY DO PEOPLE enjoy being in a club? What satisfaction do people derive from being avid sports fans? Often the sense of belonging is as meaningful as the activity itself. A strong sense of belonging banishes loneliness. Man longs to experience the joy of belonging, the joy of widening his personal life to belong to a larger one, a family. The human heart craves the joy of belonging and the sense of companionship. A warm church home can be a foretaste of Heaven. Worship Me in spirit and truth, and together we will find a warm church home.

All the believers were together and had everything in common. Acts 2:44

MAY 27 —

I Will Use You

Lord, I won't let go of You this morning until I receive Your blessing.

THERE ARE MANY people all around you who need encouragement. So many lives are unaffirmed here on the earth. Here allow Me to greet you so that you will be prepared to greet others. You must receive blessings before you are able to pass them along to others. Heaven greets you this morning to nurse your strained mind and tired body. I will use you. Smile and get others to smile with you. Laugh and prompt humor in others. Let all know that your daily hope for yourself is found only in Me. Take life from Me and share it with others.

Grace and peace to you from God our Father and the Lord Jesus Christ. Ephesians 1:2

The Cost of Being a Disciple

Jesus, break Satan's chains and help me to do only Your will.

WHATEVER THE COST, follow Me. The cost of following Me is the same for the seeker today as in My days on the earth. You must be ready to count all a loss compared with the value of following Me. You must be willing to surrender all to My plans. You must allow My influence on your life to be stronger than any earthly relationship. The cost of being a disciple is all-encompassing. Yet, it also provides the promise of eternity in Heaven and a rich and meaningful life here on the earth.

Anyone who loves their father or mother more than me is not worthy of me; anyone who loves their son or daughter more than me is not worthy of me.
Matthew 10:37

I Have Jesus' Comfort

I pray to You, Jesus. You alone can bring order out of chaos and peace out of turmoil.

THE WORLD SPEAKS of stressors: death, divorce, illness, a lost job. Whatever these forces are labeled, you must know that I have overcome them. Take My gifts from Me. My light can pierce through to earth's darkest places. My love can penetrate even to the secret hurt in a life. My comfort can console all in every situation. I can bring hope when all hope seems lost. I can give you peace that human logic cannot provide. Say today, "I have Jesus' comfort."

So do not fear, for I am with you; do not be dismayed, for I am your God. I will strengthen you and help you; I will uphold you with my righteous right hand.
Isaiah 41:10

The Coaching Phase

Lord, thank You for Your watchfulness over my family.
Keep all of us safe; guide us home. Let Your Spirit sus-
tain us and give us not only wisdom, but hope.

LET THERE BE no rush in your step, no haste to your conversations, and no worry in your tone. Let Me watch over your home. In the parable of the prodigal son, there could be told a backstory before the son departed—a time when he fought against his father's values, a time of rebellion within the home, not outside of it. As a parent, you are in the coaching phase. Let him go a little; I have him. He is under My wing and cared for in ways you cannot see. Rejoice in what you see that is praiseworthy. Celebrate all that is good. Look past what you see as ugliness and mistaken paths. Take from Me a full supply of My hope for yourself and your dear ones.

When my life was ebbing away, I remembered you, LORD, and my prayer rose to you, to your holy temple. Jonah 2:7

Jesus Guides My Way

Jesus, thank You for grace and the continual opportunity to connect with You and receive life and guidance.

TO REMAIN IN Me, you must rush back here whenever you feel depleted and lack direction. When you feel adrift and are uncertain about your next steps, return to Me. Here you are in your refuge. Here I insert My goodness back into your being and give you My direction for the day. Here, together, we push back worry about tomorrow. Leave tomorrow's guidance for tomorrow, knowing you will be led at the right time. Say today, "Jesus guides my way."

Without good direction, people lose their way.
Proverbs 11:14 MSG

JUNE 1 –
Share with Me

Lord, I feel distant from You. Help me to restore connection with You.

WHEN EARTH BONDS pull powerfully, you lose your awareness of Me. Rejuvenation springs from reconnection with Me. Reconnect with Me by talking to Me more. Let your prayer life be more than a flood of requests. Throughout the day, take the time to share with Me your gratitude, impressions, thoughts, and concerns. If you love Me more than all, it follows naturally that you would share these things with Me. I am with you through all, but there is a blessing for you in sharing your joys, pains, and observations with Me. It connects you ever closer to Me. It can turn the ordinary day into a glorious one.

And pray in the Spirit on all occasions with all kinds of prayers and requests. Ephesians 6:18

Your Daylight Breaks

Lord, grant me the hope I need this day.

OBSERVE THE GRADUAL work of sunshine on the rain-soaked lawn. The warm rays dry the wet ground. It accomplishes its work, not in a minute, not in an hour but in a morning, half a day. There is no doubt it will accomplish its work; its rays are too bright and warm. In your life the storm has raged, but your daylight breaks. I will restore, heal, bind together, and replenish. You have nothing to worry about. However, My work may occur gradually and not in an instant.

There he was transfigured before them. His face shone like the sun, and his clothes became as white as the light. Matthew 17:2

Protect Your Inner Peace

Lord, I surrender my frustrations to You; let me be all You would have me be in this situation.

UNBIND AND LET go; this is My command to you concerning those circumstances that keep you tied to unhealthy situations. Your kindness is met with hostility but harbor no negative thought. Pray for all but let go of relationships that do not benefit your inner being. Do not let guilt or concern about what others may say influence your actions. Be respectful but add distance between your life and theirs. Do not be distracted by a person I am not putting on your path. Protect your inner peace. Guard your joy.

Do not be yoked together with unbelievers. For what do righteousness and wickedness have in common? Or what fellowship can light have with darkness.
2 Corinthians 6:14

JUNE 4 –
Clear Eyes

Grant me the eyes to see Your will, big and small.

THE LEADERS THE world views as most powerful, wield a power much smaller than that of My simple-hearted followers. There is a power to a life that serves Me with undivided devotion. As My disciple, seek only to hear My voice and obey My loving commands. "'Tis the gift to be simple, 'tis a gift to be free. 'Tis a gift to come down where you ought to be" ("Simple Gifts," Joseph Brackett, 1848). So often it is not the learned and wise who serve Me the best. A man or woman with clear eyes who seeks to see the world as Heaven does, wields a power that the world's greatest would never understand. Use all the gifts you have to serve the kingdom, but the surrender of an undivided will for Heaven's use advances Heaven's aims much more than any talent or position. Small acts of service for Me far outweigh the supposedly big things done in My name that were never prompted by Heaven.

For it is God who works in you to will and to act in order to fulfill his good purpose. Philippians 2:13

This Dependent Lifestyle

Lord, let me plan this day according to Your will.

YOU SEEK A scripted day, prewritten by you before the day begins. This thinking eliminates the flow to life that you are meant to experience. Live your life continually seeking to be in sync with Me. Let the Spirit nudge you here and there. This dependent lifestyle results in joy and effectiveness as you lean on Me for strength and direction moment to moment. A rigid and pre-programed day is not My aim. Trust Me enough to be with you, and for you, in each situation as we seek to do good for Heaven. Turn to Me when you are weary and lack direction, and I will show you the way.

He gives strength to the weary and increases the power of the weak. Isaiah 40:29

Imitate My Silence

Help me know what to say in this situation.

DO NOT EXPECT to remain in unbroken accord with everyone. It is not possible. With each tinge of disagreement, seek My guidance and help. When troubles arise, turn them over to Me first and seek My instruction. Sometimes a robust word is needed to protect a loved one or the honor of Heaven. At times a gentle answer is the right response. At others, no response is required. In these instances, imitate My silence before Caiaphas and Pilate. Your only duty is to turn the matter over to Me, knowing that I fully understand you, and that nothing more is needed. No explaining. No long-winded defenses. At these moments, let the quietness and righteousness of your life speak louder than your words. Too much talk dulls you and hinders your ability to hear Me.

Jesus made no reply, not even to a single charge—to the great amazement of the governor. Matthew 27:14

You Serve a God of Light, Warmth, and Joy

Lord, I am excited to spend this early morning hour with You.

LIVING WITHOUT ME is like being in a dark garden with a dim flashlight. Some of the beauty can be seen, but most of the delights go unnoticed. Living with Me is like being in the same garden illuminated by sunlight from above revealing all the subtle hues. Could I have made the world barren of color? No, you serve a God of light, warmth, and joy. Sadly, these are all too often not reflected in My dear ones. Bring My light and life into your being every day and let it illuminate your path. I want you to be able to see all I have created for you to enjoy.

You are the light of the world. A town built on a hill cannot be hidden. Matthew 5:14

My Curative Powers

Thank You for dying for a sinner like me.

RUSH AND PANIC have overtaken you. You have no marrow within you to withstand the situation, but here with Me, all is well. Here with Me, all is made plain. Flowers drenched with dew teeter and bend, pressing their petals into mud and filth, their glory exchanged for shame. They await in knowing anticipation that the curative sun and warm, healing air will bring back their glory. Then, merry and bright, they are righted, find their way, and provide their happy purpose spreading joy and hope. Here, I provide My sun on your downcast face, changing the sickly pale to health. Arise in anticipation of My curative powers.

Consider how the wild flowers grow. They do not labor or spin. Luke 12:27

JUNE 9 –

Trace the Thread of Gold

Lord, greet me here this morning.

SEE MEANING IN life as you trace the thread of gold—My path—for you each day. All is planned. Reject all thoughts of happenstance. Look for My thread today. Along My thread, you will find the joy you are looking for. When you see it, say to yourself, "This is the Lord's thread for me." Let this refrain fill you with the thrill of My love and planning.

You make known to me the path of life; you will fill me with joy in your presence, with eternal pleasures at your right hand. Psalm 16:11

JUNE 10 –
Join with Heaven

I want Your way, Jesus.

A QUIET, HAPPY life may speak more than a preacher's long-winded sermon. A gentle response may show more discipline than tremendous sacrifice. A simple guided task may advance the kingdom more than a bold act of evangelism. When you join with Heaven, you will always find success. This success is driven from above. It may not receive the applause of men, but it will receive My seal of approval.

In everything he did he had great success, because the LORD was with him. 1 Samuel 18:14

Serve Larger Portions of My Love

Protect me and use me as You would.

THE WORLD AROUND you needs love more than you know. I see the hurt each man hides. I see the shame he hides with bravado. I see the emptiness he masks with work and busyness. Serve larger portions of My love—use a big ladle. With gracious eyes, see the uniqueness and beauty in those around you. Greet them with kind words. Dole out encouragement with a free hand. In most instances, you do not have to express your convictions; they are already known. You do not have the task of changing others; I do that. Your role is to love them and introduce them to Me, the world's Savior. Have the heart of Our Father, who wants to see all brought to Me.

A new command I give you: Love one another. As I have loved you, so you must love one another. John 13:34

Travel Light

I always believe but help me believe more.

FAITH IS THE steamroller that flattens every obstacle in your path. It levels the ground so that you can walk safely, securely, and with peace. Without faith in My power working in your life, you are overwhelmed by your own problems and cannot help your fellow man. Apply your faith in Me to each thing that vexes you so that you can travel light and be available for kingdom use. Believe in Me as your powerful Lord and Savior. By trusting, with a full dose of faith applied, you are available. When you are overwhelmed with burdens, you are on the spiritual sidelines. Live like you have a mighty Savior who guards your life.

Guard my life, for I am faithful to you; save your servant who trusts in you. You are my God. Psalm 86:2

Until Hurt Turns to Blessing

Jesus, repair me. Fix me, and I will be fixed.

THE NEED FOR healing draws you closer to Me. The Prince of Peace heals you whenever you can get near Him. Say, "My Lord is here." Stay here. What you really need is to feel My nearness, and then all is well. Let Me bring peace to your mind. Say, "My Lord is here" until hurt turns to blessing. It is the joy that comes from drawing closer to Me.

He heals the brokenhearted and binds up their wounds. Psalm 147:3

Childlike Gratitude

Lord, my soul longs to be freed from the failure-sense, shortage of supply, and meaningless work. Show up, Lord. Show up today.

CHILDLIKE GRATITUDE IS a weapon that can change the world. See My blessings in your current circumstances even if I am not ready to bring the change you seek. When My spiritual or material blessings come, then give childlike thanks. However, if they seem to be delayed, then continue to express gratitude for all the good in your life. Acknowledge that I control all. Say your thanks today for the small blessings in your life, and then you will see Me. Your lesson for the day is to let not one gift I send to you go unrecognized. Thank Me for the small things, and soon causes of joy will spring from your heart.

I will give thanks to you, Lord, with all your heart; I will tell of all your wonderful deeds. Psalm 9:1

JUNE 15 –
A Clean Soul

*Thank you, Jesus for all that you provide. In faith, I
thank you for another bestowal today.*

EVERYONE LIKES A clean house. Everyone would
also enjoy a clean soul if they knew how to obtain it.
The wonder of Christianity is that each soul who turns
to Me is fully restored and cleansed of past mistakes.
Only with Christian grace is restoration possible. Stay
here longer. Why only wash your hands when your
whole body needs to be cleansed. Say today, "Jesus
cleans my soul."

After that, he poured water into a basin and began to
wash his disciples' feet, drying them with the towel that
was wrapped around him. John 13:5

Let Me Tell Your Story

Jesus, help me find encouragement and renewal in You.

LET ME TELL your story; do not let it be told by others. Sometimes what My follower hears early in his life from a parent, sibling, classmate, or coach may resonate more than My view of his life. Focus on My love for you; this is your path to staying positive. Flush out self-doubt, shame, and criticism with My overflowing love and care for you. I see a man who is overcoming with Heaven's full supply of love and forgiveness. A man who desires to help others. A man whose best intentions are to advance the kingdom within and without. Yes, let Me tell your story.

But to each one of us grace has been given as Christ apportioned it. Ephesians 4:7

JUNE 17 –

A Beautiful Soul is the Goal

Take my heart, mind, and soul, Lord, and make it one with Yours.

SPENDING THIS TIME with Me is like a session in which a faulty, marred stone is placed with a master sculptor. He uses precise tools to perfect the piece. His movements are delicate and accurate. Rough edges are smoothed. Dark spots are made bright and clear. A beautiful design emerges. And so it is with each of My followers. A beautiful soul is the goal. Each day I show you another step you can take for the kingdom. Not all steps for Me are external. Some are in your inner being.

When Jacob awoke from his sleep, he thought, "Surely the LORD is in this place, and I was not aware of it." Genesis 28:16

Christianity Works for Me

Jesus, thank You for Your guiding hand that I know is there even when I do not see it.

STORMS MAY RAGE, but My loved ones are kept in perfect peace. You are not—at any time—subject to haphazard events. All is planned by Me in love and kindness. Say to yourself, "Christianity works for me." Say this as a reminder that My teachings prove themselves to be true. Say this to remind yourself of the inner peace I alone can provide. Say this to remind yourself that Heaven's forces intercede continually on your behalf. Say this as a reminder of who you are.

Simon Peter answered him, "Lord, to whom shall we go? You have the words of eternal life." John 6:68

JUNE 19 —
Requests from a Friend

Thank you, Jesus, that You are a friend to sinners like me.

A KING GIVES orders. The general commands his troops. I give you requests from a friend. Find in this the heart of Heaven. Nothing forced. The Father wants a voluntary, glad turning to Me each day. In that spirit go out. Say to yourself, "I always listen to My friend's requests." Have a childlike spirit that does not want to go its own way, but rather Mine.

Now if we are children, then we are heirs—heirs of God and co-heirs with Christ, if indeed we share in his sufferings in order that we may also share in his glory. Romans 8:17

Lose the Self-Doubt

Lord, help me overcome the spirit of discouragement that has weighed on me the last few days. Fill me with Your courage.

HOW I LONG to find the faith on the earth that would allow My Father's work to advance unimpeded. Faith and self-denial are keys to spiritual success as shown in the interchange with the sick boy's father in Galilee. My disciples could not help the dispirited and suicidal boy. Pray and deny yourself. Shake off the rusty parts that no longer serve your vessel. Toss them overboard, so that alighted and buoyant, you can chart a new, faster course for Me. Higher in the water. Faster across the way. Lose the self-doubt that hinders Our work. It is My power, not yours, that matters. I need you to be the soul doctor who can fix the boy when I am away. Your fault is self-doubt. See it in your life. Identify it and cast it out. Let Me transform you so that you may transform others. All things can be done through him who believes and does not doubt.

"You unbelieving generation," Jesus replied, "how long shall I stay with you? How long shall I put up with you? Bring the boy to me." Mark 9:19

JUNE 21 –
Genuineness

Lord, please forgive my waywardness.

GENUINENESS MEANS THAT you do not have to claim to be without sin. Others see the genuineness of your walk and are blessed. All men have done and seen things that they wish they had not. I can use the humble man mightily. Each day remember your need to have Me pulsating from your core and flowing into every area of your life. In this way, seek to be perfect. Your life will be marked by imperfection stretching for perfection until you reach Heaven. Christianity is a sinners-only religion.

These have come so that the proven genuineness of your faith—of greater worth than gold, which perishes even though refined by fire—may result in praise, glory and honor when Jesus Christ is revealed. 1 Peter 1:7

The Noblest Cause

Thank You for the happy baptism I was able to be a part of.

THE NOBLEST CAUSE is to bring lost sheep back to their shepherd, to help bring life to dead men. This is the Christian adventure for all My followers. It is a joyful march that has a merry rhythm, but it is not for the faint of heart. We seek to free all from the devil's strongholds. We seek to interject love, joy, and trust in the hearts of those the devil would keep in fear, loathing, and hatred. He fears the power of Heaven and knows his days are numbered. Together we fight his imps and ignoble plans. Your cause is to show man the glorious reunion available to him. Grace is an unconquerable force for good.

The seventy-two returned with joy and said, "Lord, even the demons submit to us in your name."
Luke 10:17

JUNE 23 —

Miracle Work

Jesus, I know Your ways are better than my ways.

A YIELDED WILL in a believer's life means power. When Heaven knows that you regularly substitute its will for yours, it calculates ways and means to do spiritual miracles through you. When on earth, I did the miraculous. Heaven's work is the work of miracles. I have not bestowed the gift of physical healing upon you, but I can work miracles through you when you make My will your will. Miracle work may go unnoticed by the world, but Heaven rejoices when the heart changes and loyalties realign.

Jesus looked at them and said, "With men this is impossible, but not with God; all things are possible with God." Mark 10:27

JUNE 24 –
Heaven's Melody

Lord, thank You for Your wonderful leading.

THE LEAVES DANCE in the cool wind. Securely, they are affixed to the branch. Happily, they hear Heaven's music. Joyfully, they move in their proper place. Attune your ear to catch Heaven's melody. All is well. All is forgiven. All is forgotten. All the pieces are falling into place. Say, "I love Jesus with all my heart." Let this be the heavenly melody you hear.

Come, let us sing for joy to the LORD; let us shout aloud to the Rock of our salvation. Psalm 95:1

A Consecrated Personality

Jesus, help me to hear the full message of the new life available only through You.

LEARN FROM ME another lesson drawn from surrendering to Me. When you live with Me in complete submission, you allow Me to draw out the personal image of God uniquely placed inside of you. There is a joy to be found in the discovery of the person Heaven intended you to be. In this process, you will find added impact for the kingdom. Simplicity and genuineness have a weight of influence. Let this day draw out the best version of you as you abide in Me. Live this day with Me and let Me reveal more of your consecrated personality. It is the personality your spirit will retain in Heaven for all eternity. It is genuine and observable by both the saved and unsaved. Rejoice in this hope that is available to all.

"Go, stand in the temple courts," he said, "and tell the people all about this new life." Acts 5:20

JUNE 26 —
A Thousand Callings

Put me where I can do the most good.

YOUTH SEARCH FOR the one overriding calling for their lives. Heaven yearns to provide a thousand callings. Believers seek that one ministry title for themselves. Heaven wants them to realize that they are dearly loved sons and daughters. There is tremendous power to the Holy Spirit's leading, but so few stop and listen. The world races ahead, and so do many of My dear ones. The Spirit hopes to intercede and advance the kingdom but waits for an invitation, a receptive soul, and a listening ear.

You did not choose me, but I chose you and appointed you so that you might go and bear fruit—fruit that will last—and so that whatever you ask in my name the Father will give you. John 15:16

JUNE 27 –
A Deep Calm

Lord, I accept Your will and acknowledge that You are powerful enough to do everything.

CALM IS THE result of trust in My power and care. It allows you to be pleasant when things do not go as you expected. There should be no rush with My disciples. Rush indicates a fear that there is not enough time to accomplish what is needed. Rush shows you are relying on your own ability and cleverness. Rush casts a slur on My provision and protection. Say, "He will take care of this. This I know." Let this refrain build in you a deep calm and an impenetrable shield around you.

Those who trust in the LORD are like Mount Zion, which cannot be shaken but endures forever.
Psalm 125:1

You Must Follow Me

Help me find Your presence where there is joy and peace.

THE SINFUL HEART craves for more. Some crave for more in the form of clothes, cars, boats, or homes. It is easy to feel sorry for yourself when you crave for more. This places self at the forefront and gives the enemy play in your life. Have I not promised you joy in My presence and treasures at My right hand? Why do you seek more and allow the devil a foothold? You envy the joy you see in others, a joy that you find elusive. My words to you are the same as those I spoke at breakfast to Peter by the Sea of Galilee: "*You must follow Me.*" I put in you the spirit that is perfect for you, the spirit that pushes you back to Me in your times of need. Follow Me and learn ever more to live within My sight where there is joy and meaningful work.

Jesus answered, "If I want him to remain alive until I return, what is that to you? You must follow me." John 21:22

JUNE 29 –
Perfect Timing

Grant me the wisdom I need to know how to proceed.

I WAS BORN on the earth at the right time. Through the Father's wisdom, I was born with perfect timing to save man. Roman peace afforded the conditions in which the kingdom could advance throughout the world. My act of ultimate kindness for all had to occur at the right time. And so it is for each person who turns to Me. Do not over pursue. At times the best outreach is to be a known fixture others can count on in their time of need. As I prompt you, act. However, let the timing be Mine. Let the timing be perfect.

In the time of those kings, the God of heaven will set up a kingdom that will never be destroyed, nor will it be left to another people. Daniel 2:44

View Silence Differently

Meet me here this morning, Lord.

VIEW SILENCE WITH Me differently. Sense in it, not emptiness and lack of form, but warmth and fullness of love. This is how Heaven affirms you. This is the rich abiding I promised to all who would put Me at the center of their lives. Let rich silence with Me soak deeply into your inner being. Each man longs to be affirmed and made to feel worthy in this way.

Let my meditation be pleasing to him; as for me, I shall be glad in the Lord. Psalm 104:34 NASB

JULY 1 –

Little Else Matters

Lord, help me to be disciplined in replacing worry with trust.

YOU ARE OF little use to the kingdom when you are full of the worries of this life. Worries are common and plentiful. They attack each man according to his unique nature. You are focusing on unimportant things. "Who cares?" and "So what?" These refrains can be more than a careless man's indifference to the world around him. With eyes fixed on Me and the eternal life that has been given to you, say to the world's concerns, "What do I care?" Be indifferent to the world's aims and noise, which can be a relentless downward pull on your soul. Love Me with all your heart. Love those I put on your path. Little else matters.

Jesus said to him, "Let the dead bury their own dead, but you go and proclaim the kingdom of God." Luke 9:60

JULY 2 –
I Am Here

Lord, I seek renewed hope this morning.

MY MESSAGE TO you is, "I am here." The problem is not the absence of My presence, but your inability to sense it. Worrisome thoughts, base distractions—these veil your view of Me. Soul starvation is the result of a soul's inability to feast on the divine pleasures from My table: love, joy, peace, and contentment, along with meaningful work. Let your soul drink deep draughts of My being, and it lives. Say to yourself today, "He is here."

And surely I am with you always, to the very end of the age. Matthew 28:20

Life is Difficult for Everyone

Jesus, thank You for being with me this morning; I feel dull and empty.

NEVER COMPARE YOURSELF to others. No one's life on this troubled earth is carefree. Here is a trustworthy saying that deserves full acceptance: life is difficult for everyone. It is sinful for you to think another's life is easier than your own. This subtle sin is the feeling, the pride in thinking, that your life is harder than theirs. This arrogant thinking puts you in the place of God. How do you know what's in another man's heart? What do you know about his inner struggles? This tool of the evil one carries with it a false humility and puffs up thoughts of yourself. Know that in this world all will have trouble. The only real solution, as you have bravely found, is to seek Me at all costs every day. I am your great reward and helper.

Each one should test their own actions. Then they can take pride in themselves alone, without comparing themselves to someone else, for each one should carry their own load. Galatians 6:4–5

Overflowing Peace

Lord, help me to serve and encourage others today.

OVERFLOWING PEACE IN full supply is available for all. Each soul requires a continuous refilling of peace in full measure, a filling to the brim, a bubbling over. Here on earth you must take time to obtain what you need from Heaven's open hand. There are no substitutes to long stays in My healing presence. In today's microwave society, you still need crock-pot meals. Stay and rest in My company to soothe tired nerves, body strain, and a frazzled mind. Awaken your spiritual senses to taste and see Heaven's plentiful supply of choice offerings, the best ingredients from its storehouse of goods. Use your family's gift of hospitality today to help soothe those bruised by the enemy. Say to yourself, "His love and care protects us; the enemy has no place here."

You prepare a table before me in the presence of my enemies. You anoint my head with oil; my cup overflows. Psalm 23:5

Be Content Now!

Lord, my mind rushes here and there with distractions. Give peace to my mind, joy to my heart, and godly steps to my feet.

YOU SEE THE gray squirrel with the fluffy tail; he is at peace in his backyard home. You should be content in your own backyard. Like Paul, learn the secret of being content whatever the situation. Do not seek to be content tomorrow; be content now! Be content so that Heaven can use you. Be content so that you can live comfortably with yourself, filled with grace and peace. Be content so that you can draw others to Me. Discontentment spurs your inner rumblings—you are discontent with your financial and work situation. Believe in Me and My power to make all things new. Say to yourself, "I'm content now." And so you make yourself available to Me and My work.

I am not saying this because I am in need, for I have learned to be content whatever the circumstances. Philippians 4:11

Tangents and Worthless Tasks

Lord, help me when I feel distracted and far from Your path for me.

TANGENTS AND WORTHLESS tasks can crowd out the risen life—life with Me. I want you to do all those things that Heaven wants you to do, but I also want you to do *only* those things that Heaven wants you to do. This involves a consecrated personality and dedication to a heavenly-ordained schedule. It is the life that springs from listening to only one voice. This should be the goal for all believers. Work on your moment-to-moment guidance to make this a reality in your life. You rely too heavily on your morning time with Me. Evolve your walk with Me so that I can use you more. Practice your faith during the day so that you can sense My presence. Hear Me and know your next steps. Allow your connection with Me to show you all I want you to do but also allow it to exclude those things that are not part of your walk with Me. There is a power that results from only doing those things Heaven asks you to do.

When they came to the border of Mysia, they tried to enter Bithynia, but the Spirit of Jesus would not allow them to. Acts 16:7

Christian Charm

In this quiet, speak to me, my Creator-Redeemer. Show me Your excellent way.

THERE IS NO charm like Christian charm. My charm is not based on good looks or stylish dress. It does not emanate from career success or monetary gain. My charm is rooted in grace. It is the feeling that the God of wonders removes all mistakes and errors. It is the sense that all good things have been given to you freely. My charm conquers guilt and shame. It puts the smile back on the despondent. It lifts the downtrodden out of the mud. It is the universal gift offered to all nations. It reaches from border to border, sea to sea. Take My charm with you into the day. Use it to influence the world for Me. Say today, "I have His charm."

Though your sins are like scarlet, they shall be white as snow. Isaiah 1:18

Trust and Hope Are Your Most Valued Possessions

Help me overcome the fears that assail and the cares that trouble me, especially those with work and money. Help the real me to be solidly hidden in that secret spiritual place with You.

YOU ARE PASSING through a storm. There are bleak conditions all around: thunder booms, lightning strikes, and the rain falls. The roof may leak. The shutters may break free. You sense your short fuse and the tension within. Keep your faith in the storm. Trust and hope are your most valued possessions now. Guidance from Me each day will provide superior wisdom and the right steps. Say to yourself, "I am protected and guided." Continue your day with trust and unlimited hope. This storm will lift and move on. Sunshine and calm will return.

Then they cried out to the LORD in their trouble, and he brought them out of their distress. Psalm 107:28

JULY 9 –

Your Key to Successful Living

Lord, help me with this difficult decision I must make today.

BOW YOUR HEAD and let Me bless you. You are God's son, and I am proud of you. Let Me pull bitterness and angst from you. In their place, take My joy and peace. To be controlled by the Spirit, you must have a yielded will, not to the passions and storms of this life, but to the gentle, quiet voice that affirms you and guides your day. Your key to successful living today is hearing that still small voice. Your conscious can tell you right from wrong, but only My voice can tell you the best choice between two good things. I never force My way into anyone's affairs. I must be invited in—even if I stand at the door and knock.

Here I am! I stand at the door and knock. If anyone hears my voice and opens the door, I will come in and eat with that person, and they with me. Revelation 3:20

Be Transformed by Recurring Gratitude

Thank you, Jesus, for new starts, friendships, and adventures.

SHAKE OFF THE drudgery and burdens that come with self-doubt and worry. Replace these with praise for Me, thus establishing your connection with Heaven. Overpower your mind with your will. Flood your mind with thanks to Me. Chase away doubt, fear, and temptations with joyful thoughts. You are what you continually think about. Let your inward being, and even outward appearance, be transformed by recurring gratitude. See the good in all you meet.

For as he thinks in his heart, so is he. Proverbs 23:7 NKJV

Gratitude As a Weapon

Help me to see causes for thankfulness.

USE GRATITUDE AS a weapon today. Thank endlessly. Set your mind here, and all else will follow in its proper place. When you do not feel grateful, it is the perfect time to practice the sacrifice of thanksgiving. Then you will think clearly and see My face. Let your mind be the master over all your feelings. You will see I do My part. I always do My part. The clouds will lift. The rain will dry up. Heaven's sunlight will reach your path.

For although they knew God, they neither glorified him as God nor gave thanks to him; but their thinking became futile and their foolish hearts were darkened. Romans 1:21

JULY 12 –
A Relentless Search

Lord, be with me. I invite You in. Cleanse me, make me whole, and send me out to serve You.

TODAY IS A new day. I wash away the disappointments and regrets of yesterday. Remember them no more. Today is new and fresh. There are two steps necessary for you as you begin this day. First, start with a relentless search to know My will. Second, desire to establish a reputation with Heaven as a faithful servant who obeys. These steps are what makes My followers joyful and effective. Let My grace soften the blows when you fall short.

He replied, "Blessed rather are those who hear the word of God and obey it." Luke 11:28

A Source of Joy

Lord, watch over me and give me Your blessing.

SHARE YOUR MATERIAL blessings with many. Share, share, share. The habit of generous giving can be a great source of joy. Seek for people and situations that draw your sympathy and give with a large hand. If you can, deliver the blessing anonymously, knowing that I see it. You will soon have spiritual blessings to share and offer to others. All is well and falling into place.

A generous person will prosper; whoever refreshes others will be refreshed. Proverbs 11:25

JULY 14 –
Heaven's Teachings

Lord, show me the spiritual fix I need today.

THE DRIBBLE OF the world's wisdom is at odds with Heaven's teachings. My teachings are often in stark contrast to earthly psychology, philosophy, and self-help instruction. The world shouts, "Be smarter, funnier, wittier, and more assertive." It demands that you plan more and that you fret out the details of your life. The kingdom calls you to give up all and serve Heaven for all its worth. Heaven beckons you to live for the other person. A meek soul wields Heaven's power. A humble personality endears itself to others. A contrite heart benefits the kingdom.

He must become greater; I must become less. John 3:30

Christian Flavor to Your Life

Lord, change me this morning in this time I get to spend with You.

TIME SPENT ALONE with Me is needed to keep you spiritually fresh. Here I add the salt to your soul that purifies you from the mistakes of yesterday and adds Christian flavor to your life today. Say to yourself, "I have been with Jesus." Too many bland Christians present Me to the world as ineffective, dull, and stale. Be distinct. Be salty. In order to add My salt to your life, you only need to sit and be with Me. Sometimes the words may be few, but this time together cannot help but alter your inner being. It is an inevitable result.

You are the salt of the earth. But if the salt loses its saltiness, how can it be made salty again? Matthew 5:13

Take Adventures with Me

Shake the dullness from my spirit and the dryness from my bones.

A LIFE OF faith is not always the safe path. It's an adventure. The predictable path of many who profess to follow Me is not the path I would have for them. Take adventures with Me. I will not overwhelm you. I seek to draw out the best in each of My followers, and what I believe they can accomplish is far greater than what they can imagine. Trade in your low-mist dreams for the glory I have in mind. Let me spur you on to the spiritual successes I have planned. Step by step, walk with Me as I direct you. Have the gentle spirit that smiles toward Heaven and says, "Lord, have Your way."

Have I not commanded you? Be strong and courageous. Do not be afraid; do not be discouraged, for the LORD your God will be with you wherever you go."- Joshua 1:9

View Yourself As a Spiritual Being

Lord, let me draw the lesson You would have me to learn from this situation.

LOOK DEEP INTO the woods. See the rays of light piercing through to the mysterious dark places. View yourself as a spiritual being, lodged in human form. This is a key to unlocking spiritual power. The spirit world is alive and surrounds you in the unseen. It is a living and vivid reality. A soul, or a group of souls, can connect with that world any time. Forces for good and evil abound. Be a weapon of My light. Help Me to shine Heaven's brilliance into the dark places of your life and the world around you. Let My spiritual power flow through you to remove the shackles and chains of the dark forces of evil.

So we fix our eyes not on what is seen, but on what is unseen, since what is seen is temporary, but what is unseen is eternal. 2 Corinthians 4:18

Replenish Your Courage

Lord, I seek Your sanity and order when my life is troubled, and I am worried.

GLAD TURNINGS TO Me in the morning and throughout the day replenish your courage. You are worn out from fighting the same old fights. Turn to Me in prayer with full confidence that I will revive you. Stay with Me for a while, and you will arise brave and courageous. Through eyes of faith, see Me, and your courage is restored. Make effort to sense My presence with you today, and you will have much courage.

Finally, be strong in the LORD and in his mighty power. Ephesians 6:10

JULY 19 –
God Is Good

Lord, help me to be bigger in this circumstance and respond as You would have me to.

IN A FALLEN world, you can rely on the fact that God is good. When the ship tosses in the raging storm far from shore, its captain sees the lighthouse and directs his crew safely home. God is good. Let this refrain be the beacon of light you need to navigate this life. God is good. You will always have trouble in this world. God is good. Material supply will come and go. God is good. Your closest friends are sinners who will let you down. God is good. Guidance sometimes seems to tarry when you need it the most. Carry on, knowing God is good.

"Why do you call me good?" Jesus answered. "No one is good—except God alone." Mark 10:18

See Yourself As I See You

I come to You this morning, knowing You will accept me and lift me up.

TIRED AND CONFUSED, you come to Me for rest and direction. In this life, you will have inner struggles. Sometimes you are the saint. Sometimes you are the sinner. Here, back with Me, I sort out the tangled thoughts and feelings welled up inside of you. I show you the path back to where you should be. See yourself as I see you, and your spirit will be lifted. There is not a moment when you are not loved by Me. Arise from this time together as a fit and ready tool to lay by your Master's hand. Rest with Me until you are refilled with My joy and calm. Quiet suggestions will spring forth. Noble tasks will be laid on your heart.

Therefore, if anyone is in Christ, he is a new creation; old things have passed away; behold, all things have become new. 2 Corinthians 5:17 NKJV

All the Confirmation You Need

Thank you, Lord, that each day I get to start again.

I PROVIDE THE soft and steady rain that washes away the dirt and grime. I give you the fresh starts you need. As a man, I provide all the confirmation you need. In Me you have wholeness and completeness. Without Me you are needy and lack love. With Me you can be a giver to your wife, children, and friends. Complete in Me, you can truly go and serve.

For in Christ all the fullness of the Deity lives in bodily form, and in Christ you have been brought to fullness. He is the head over every power and authority. Colossians 2:9–10

JULY 22 –
Connecting with Others

Lord, help me to love others the way You did while on earth.

SEE OTHERS AS they are, not as you think they should be. Give your emphasis to connecting with others instead of convicting them of some truth. Many needy souls have been pushed further from Me by My followers' mistaken belief that they should share their convictions. Convictions shared outside the warmth of relationship often speak condemnation. Think in terms of the other man's interests and needs. Be a courteous Christian interested in the other person's well-being and happiness.

Rather, in humility value others above yourselves, not looking to your own interests but each of you to the interests of the others. Philippians 2:3–4

JULY 23 –
A Properly Ordered Life

Jesus, thank You for the beauty I see all around me.

SPEND MORE TIME outside. Hear testimony about Me from the stars and sky. See My glory in sunshine's defeat of darkness. Hear My melody in the songs of birds and the chatter of crickets. Absorb My beauty from the lush shades of leaves and the even blades of grass. All nature is properly ordered by Me. No chaos or confusion reigns here. See in nature this lesson for you now: place Me first, and all else falls into place. Seek to help others put their lives in proper order by putting Me first. This is the genesis of a properly ordered life.

The heavens declare the glory of God; the skies proclaim the work of his hands. Day after day they pour forth speech; night after night they reveal knowledge. Psalm 19:1–2

Heaven Calling | 229

JULY 24 –
Be Changed

Lord, grant me peace of mind.

ALLOW SUFFICIENT TIME for the healing and re-filling of your own soul before you attempt to help others. Do not rush forward. Wait to be prompted by Me. The quality of Christian work is more important than the quantity of work done in My name. You must have peace in your heart before you can share it with others. Joy must be internal before it can affect a crowd. Acceptance must be felt inwardly before you can fully embrace others. Goodness must be found before it can be given. Be changed before you attempt to change others.

I will give you a new heart and put a new spirit within you; I will remove from you your heart of stone and give you a heart of flesh. Ezekiel 36:26

A Time to Run and Accomplish

Lord, manage me; help me prioritize my responsibilities.

A PACIFIER FOR the baby, a bike for the boy, a cane for the old man, but running shoes for the middle-aged man! A time to run and accomplish. Take the patience you need from Me to make it through this busy life stage. No aimless pursuits. I am leading you into new situations and adventures for the sake of influence. Change the world through subtle influences. Change the world as a humble man on his knees. Help make Me real and vibrant today. In Me you have a friend who not only knows everything about the race you are in, but one who also runs it with you.

Therefore I do not run like someone running aimlessly; I do not fight like a boxer beating the air. 1 Corinthians 9:26

JULY 26 –
Return to Me

Lord, remove from me the deadness I feel.

THE DEADNESS YOU feel is your alarm to return to Me. When you lose the thrill for life, return to Me. When you hear deadness in your voice, return to Me. When you are without dreams, return to Me. When you are desperate, return to Me. When the evil one has stolen your joy, return to Me. Find personal revival today. Live with Me at the center of your being. Allow Me the joy of supplying you with all you need for a full and abundant life here on earth.

When the apostles returned, they reported to Jesus what they had done. Then he took them with him and they withdrew by themselves to a town called Bethsaida. Luke 9:10

Be Preoccupied with Me

Jesus, bless Your Holy name. Let me know and love You more today. Let me receive Your perfect will with thanksgiving.

SO MUCH OF what occupies your mind is insignificant. Become preoccupied with nobler thoughts and higher plans. Be preoccupied with Me. I have much planned for you. I will never cease to plan good and exciting things for you. I am your ever-present, ever-active Lord and Savior. I will never fail you. I will never depart from you. Engross yourself with Me, and the ignoble, insignificant things will fade away.

His disciples remembered that it is written, "Zeal for your house will consume me." John 2:17

The Surprising Power of Grace

Lord, thank You for the grace and life that I can find only in You.

EVEN WHEN YOU watch for the early rays of the dawn, they still appear unexpectedly, flashing light across your horizon. It is the same with the grace I warmly extend each day to My followers. You know it will come, but its effect is still startling. And so it was when My grace was first provided. Even though My death on the cross was prophesized for thousands of years, no man was prepared for the thunderous power of grace from the cross when I said, "It is finished." Together we go today to tell of the surprising power of grace. You have more work to do for Me, more lives to influence, more minutes to serve Heaven.

His splendor was like the sunrise; rays flashed from his hand, where his power was hidden. Habakkuk 3:4

Meaningful Work

Thank you that You are near and that You hear me.

YOUR PATH IS planned. It is filled with meaningful work for the kingdom. Do not be discouraged if I give you a season of wanting different work, a time of watching for it. Want and watch in peace, full of trust in your kind King. Rest and remain in Me. This is your current service for Me. Your joy, though elusive, will reappear. Do not doubt. Do not fear. Do not lose hope. Say today, "I accept all that He allows."

I will be good for those servants whose master finds them watching when he comes. Truly I tell you, he will dress himself to serve, will have them recline at the table and will come and wait on them. Luke 12:37

JULY 30 –

Be in the Spiritual Battle

Jesus, I lay my will before Your throne. Help me to make sense of yesterday's events.

FIGHT TODAY WITH praise. Be in the spiritual battle. You do not need special spiritual insight; your spiritual need is to have a grateful heart. Trust Me in this time by giving Me thanks. Give Me a grateful heart, and I will reward you with a sense of protection and peace. Thank Me for the blessings in your life that you see; thank Me also for your blessings in the unseen. You have eternity to live in Heaven.

A cheerful heart is good medicine, but a crushed spirit dries up the bones. Proverbs 17:22

JULY 31 –
Your Quiet Savior

I trust You with all, Jesus. Let me sense Your nearness.

I AM HERE. The haze from your daily activities hinders your view of your quiet Savior. But I am here all the same. Here with Me, the fog of despair and the clouds of doubt are lifted and replaced with sunshine and warm breezes. Say to yourself today, "I have Him; I have all I need." There is not a moment you are not loved by Me.

The Lord your God is with you, the Mighty Warrior who saves. He will take great delight in you; in his love he will no longer rebuke you, but will rejoice over you with singing. Zephaniah 3:17

AUGUST 1 –
A Work in Progress

Lord, save me from my many faults.

HEAVEN'S GIFTS TO you today are patience and grace. You are a work in progress, developing into the man I would have you to be. Stone upon stone. Obedience to Me followed by more obedience. Surrender to Me followed by more surrender. Feel the thrill of seeing My will done in your life. Do not waste time viewing the places on your path where you have stumbled. What does that gain you? See the beauty of Heaven's creativity played out in your life as you partner with Me. Apply My tender patience to your life and accept the warm grace I have for your imperfect, but genuine, walk with Me.

Be diligent in these matters; give yourself wholly to them, so that everyone may see your progress. 1 Timothy 4:15

A God-Guided Life

When my days are tough, remind me that You are in control.

WHEN THE STORM rages, know the joy of a God-guided life. Do you not see that this is the only way for man to live? This is how he was created by Me to live. Let Me remove the mountains of doubt, fear, and sin and guide you in the way you should go. I wish to give you a life spent—not tirelessly doing all things, but carefully performing the tasks I give you. Every day surrendered to Me is part of a God-guided life.

Take my yoke upon you and learn from me for I am gentle and humble in heart, and you will find rest for your souls. Matthew 11:29

Safeguard Your Spiritual Home

Let me abide in You. With Your power, eradicate all that is not according to Your will from my nature.

SEE YOUR QUIET times as necessary to safeguard your spiritual home. Pump spiritual air into your being so that spiritual currents seep from you, from a heart filled with joy and thanksgiving. The overflow prevents the negative and the evil from entering your being. Thus, you keep your peace and calm protected, separate and safe from the world around you, impenetrable to the devil's forces. Let a smile show the world that your true joy is tucked away safely with Me.

So then, just as you received Christ Jesus as Lord, continue to live your lives in him, rooted and built up in him, strengthened in the faith as you were taught, and overflowing with thankfulness. Colossians 2:6–7

AUGUST 4 –
Love Is Here

I claim from You the love that I do not have.

MY PRESENCE IS love's presence in your life. Love is the catalyst that changes you, your family, and the world. Love sent Me to earth. Love pulled Me back to Heaven. Love wins and is stronger than all else. Let My love and light fill you and let evil run to distant lands. Say to yourself today and always, "Love is here."

A new command I give you: Love one another. As I have loved you, so you must love one another. John 13:34

The Joy of Expecting Good

Lord, I feel misplaced at work. Fill me with joy and peace, and I will be complete.

BLAST YOUR WAY through the doldrums of today with thanks and praise. Charge the Spirit's power in you with gratitude. Snuff out doubts and fears with the cover of prayer. Gratitude builds up an overflow of thanksgiving in your nature that changes you. It changes what you say and how you say it. It can be seen and felt by those near you. Through this new mind-set, obtain the joy of expecting good to happen in your life and the lives of those around you.

And whatever you do, whether in word or deed, do it all in the name of the Lord Jesus, giving thanks to God the Father through him. Colossians 3:17

Captain of Your Life

Lord, I look only to You for help and salvation. What are my next steps? Give me a rung to step upon, a life-line to grab.

I MUST BE the captain of each soul who desires to follow Me. A captain has absolute authority of the ship. Those are also the terms for all who would come to Me. Submit to Me as the captain of your life. I am a captain who can always be trusted. My motives are always pure and loving. My decisions are always right and wise. But, I can only be your captain if you give Me the helm. Release your grasp of the wheel. I can only be on board as the captain, never a shipmate. If you have hold of the wheel of your life or if you give it to someone else, I must leave the ship. Yes, come on board. What an adventure we will have. What excitement! What safety! What purpose!

Whoever finds their life will lose it, and whoever loses their life for my sake will find it. Matthew 10:39

AUGUST 7 –
The Light of This World

Thank you, Lord, that You are a rich giver. Speak life and truth to me this morning.

GOD IS LOVE and light. In Him, the Father, there is no darkness. But, in the world there is night, darkness, and pain. Your only hope is to be led by the light of this world. Those who lived in the Dark Ages are thought to have lived in a time of desperation, ignorance, and barbarism. Those who live today without Me are in a spiritually dark age. If My light does not shine forth from the lives of My followers, where can the world turn to for hope? My followers have been much maligned, but the places in the world where they have not had influence are the most desperate and cold. Let the light that shines from Heaven be on your face today. Be a dependable reflection of My love and care for the world.

Many, LORD, are asking, "Who will bring us prosperity?" Let the light of your face shine on us. Psalm 4:6

Continual Companionship

Thank You, Jesus, for the calm that comes only through prayer.

DEVELOP YOUR SPIRITUAL sixth sense. Go beyond what you can see and hear. Say, "I sense Jesus' presence here and now." Your whole life is altered when you are aware of Me. Know the joy and freedom that life with Me brings. The frightened child is at peace when his mother has him in her arms. A person's long drive is joyful when accompanied by a close friend. Take another lesson from this. My followers' temptations are overcome when they are fully aware of My presence. Choose this life—a life of joy, happiness, and meaning. A life of continual companionship with Me.

Never will I leave you; never will I forsake you. Hebrews 13:5

A Sound Mind

Lord, remake me this morning. Perform a miracle in my heart. Cleanse me of annoyance and frustration. Replace these temptations with Your love, joy, and peace.

WITHOUT CONNECTION WITH Me, each soul lives in pain and suffering. There are no exceptions. Only the mind that is surrendered to Me is truly sound. A sound mind produces sane thoughts that promote healthy decisions. A diseased mind produces diseased thoughts and unhealthy actions. True life and health are found only in Me, the Creator of mind, body, and soul.

Jesus answered, "I am the way and the truth and the life. No one comes to the Father except through me." John 14:6

AUGUST 10 –
Watch Your Lifeline

Jesus, You are the most important person in my life. Thank You for giving me every good thing. Bless my family and show me the next good thing.

PEACE OF MIND is difficult for man to acquire. Many seek solace in My awe-inspiring creation through hiking, fishing, boating, gardening, and horseback riding. Time spent outdoors nourishes the soul, bringing it spiritual minerals necessary for health. Sunlight is one of My finest gifts to mankind. As you know, there is a deeper connection with Me that each soul craves and so few find—the joy of the created reconnecting with the Creator. Spiritual malnourishment is an epidemic plaguing man. Soul-starved men and women run the world. When the Son of Man comes, will He find faith on this earth? Your intimate time with Me is not only a lifeline for yourself, but also serves as a lifeline for others. Watch your lifeline; keep it first and foremost, daily and hourly. Save both yourself and those near to you.

Watch your life and doctrine closely. Persevere in them, because if you do, you will save both yourself and your hearers. 1 Timothy 4:16

Dare to Dream

Show me the way, Lord, to Your joyful work. Lead me down Your paths.

DARE TO DREAM and receive inspiration from Me. To influence others is to change the world. My aim is to change the world through My followers. Think bigger; you are following My inspirations, not your own. When you push aside petty self-thoughts and allow My power to work through you, you can be an effective instrument for Heaven's use. If each of My dear ones would surrender themselves fully to Me as they are—with all their faults, blemishes, and sinful tendencies—I could put them where they could do the most good for Me. False humility is sinful because it is selfish and causes self-focus. It is through My power that My followers accomplish mighty works for Me.

In the last days, God says, I will pour out my Spirit on all people. Your sons and daughters will prophesy, your young men will see visions, your old men will dream dreams. Acts 2:17

A Strong Sense of Family

*Jesus, thank You for this beautiful summer morning.
I give You thanks for it and Your presence and grace.
Help me to have the heart and mind that You would
want for me.*

ISOLATION IS ONE of the evil one's strongest weapons. It is the opposite of a strong sense of family and belonging. My followers are adopted sons and daughters. They are part of a heavenly family. They belong to the kingdom. Continue to build family in your home, church, and with your friends. My love and acceptance builds a home for all.

God sets the lonely in families, he leads out the prisoners with singing, but the rebellious live in a sunscorched land. Psalm 68:6

You Are Wonderfully Led

Thank you, Lord, for being specific and careful. Your planning is the opposite of whim and happenstance.

WALK ALONG THE path I have set for you. It is not in short sprints that the journey is covered, but in careful marches. Ask yourself, "What is His path for me today?" When you make Me Lord, you are in position to receive My daily plans for you. See in this My injunction to My disciples to be childlike. I lift the worry of planning and calculating your own path. Leave all of that to Me today and every day. Rejoice in the knowledge that you are wonderfully led.

From one man he made all the nations, that they should inhabit the whole earth; and he marked out their appointed times in history and the boundaries of their lands. Acts 17:26

AUGUST 14 —
Your Shield

Lord, save me from all that depresses me.

USE YOUR FAITH in Me as a shield. Envision a metal shield for your use, a barrier between you and all that bothers you. See it as powerful and effective. Feel invincible as I, your shield, go with you to each appointment, each task. Place Me between you and all that you face. When you walk in faith in Me, nothing can harm you.

The Lord is my strength and my shield; my heart trusts in him, and he helps me. Psalm 28:7

Refreshed by My Grace

*Jesus, speak to me in Your mercy, and I am found
again.*

BREAK THE CHAINS that bind you to earth's sordid
affairs. Hatred, envy, greed, and lust—all these bind
men, even Heaven-bound men, to the low mist of earth.
Love, joy, and peace—these you will have in plentiful
supply as you live near Me and for Me. The acceptance
of My forgiveness is the key that draws the fruit of the
Spirit into your life. Accept Heaven's warm embrace.
Accept the grace that is sufficient for you—the grace
that is all you need and all that you really want. Let My
warm grace calm you and make you whole. Say today,
"I am refreshed by His grace."

Repent, then, and turn to God, so that your sins may
be wiped out, that times of refreshing may come from
the Lord. Acts 3:19

AUGUST 16 –
Be a Peacemaker

Jesus, reveal to me what You would have me hear. Whether my days be many or few, let me be the best version of me I can be and have the most influence for You.

MY MISSION TODAY, as when I lived in bodily form on the earth, is to return each soul to our Father through Me. This is what it means to be a peacemaker. To be effective as a peacemaker, you must be meek and act as I direct you. So many lost souls have been hindered in approach to Me by the words of men. The babel of men does not advance Heaven's aims. I alone can show you where and how to act. I alone can help you hit the mark with those who seek Me.

Blessed are the peacemakers, for they will be called children of God. Matthew 5:9

AUGUST 17 –

Come to Your Senses

Lord, help me with the frustration I feel this morning.

COMPLETE SURRENDER OF your will to Mine is your spiritual key today. Your frustrations are not from outward circumstances, but from within. You struggle to accept My will for you. You long for things and for paths that are not what I want for you. You struggle until you come to your senses and hear My voice. Imitate My humility on the earth, and your spirit will be renewed. Say today, "I accept all of His good and pleasing will." Do this and win the battle and revive your spirit.

Going a little farther, he fell with his face to the ground and prayed, "My Father, if it is possible, may this cup be taken from me. Yet not as I will, but as you will." Matthew 26:39

AUGUST 18 —
The Ones You Love

Thank You for the sun coming up today. Thank You for the light that banishes darkness. I pray a specific prayer for Your blessing on our daughter today and help for me as I struggle with her going away to college.

THE SUN IS up, and I am up too. I do not slumber or rest. Trust that the center of My will is the safest and most blessed place. That is where she is. Wholesome and healthy. Friendly and warm. She has landed where she wants to be and where I have planned for her. Think of My heartache for those souls who do not know Me and who wreck their lives with sin. Empathize with Me as I long for their return home. You have not lost her; she is right around the corner. Your feelings are honest, true, and right. They will not overwhelm you this day or any other day. You have done your best with her, and you are not through yet. She is blessed. Say today, "All according to His good plan. We are blessed. She is blessed." There is no greater joy than seeing the ones you love, love Me and following My plan for them.

It has given me great joy to find some of your children walking in the truth, just as the Father commanded us. 2 John 1:4

AUGUST 19 –
Your Special Anointment

Thank You for this waiting time with You. Help me to rejoice along the way in all things this day.

THIS IS YOUR private time to be with Me, a time to receive your special anointment for the day. This is how I want each of My children to live and discover My purposes for their lives. Do you see the potential in each life that lives with Me? This is the way to tap into the Spirit's power. In this way, each of My disciples can discover their true self—who I intended them to be. This God-led life allows you to feel that your cup overflows with My blessings and gifts. Live day to day, from one quiet time to the next. Open your spiritual eyes daily to see all I see in you and all I wish to accomplish through you.

As for you, the anointing you received from him remains in you, and you do not need anyone to teach you. But, as his anointing teaches you about all things and as that anointing is real, not counterfeit—just as it has taught you, remain in him. 1 John 2:27

Let Joy and Celebration Mark the Day

Lord, I am overwhelmed with sadness. I am so proud of my son, and I know he is ready for college, but I will miss him tremendously.

I KNOW YOU need a heart massage today. You feel the hurt of separation from one you love dearly. You will always be together through the Spirit. You will spend eternity with him too. I have your boy safely in My care. Many and marvelous are My plans for him. Happy and secure are he and his light-hearted roommate. Varied and vivid will be their adventures. Helpful and humble is the spirit they take to campus. Loving and lonely are the parents back home. You are not far in spirit, nor in distance. Let joy and celebration mark the day.

Children are a heritage from the LORD, offspring a reward from him. Psalm 127:3

AUGUST 21 –

Keep in Step with the Spirit

Jesus, I praise You for Your impact on this world. Help me be led in all things by Your Spirit.

HOW IS IT possible for mortal man to keep in step with the Spirit? The Holy Spirit can be like a cool breeze that refreshes your soul. Its light touch on your face offers encouragement and the solace needed when the world is harsh. You can walk in sync with the Spirit with absolute surrender to My will. Quickly realize when your will is not My will. Listen to the Spirit's prompting in all things. The Spirit prompts acts of kindness, love, and friendship toward all. The Spirit rejoices in honest and humble acts. The Spirit reveres selfless thinking and genuine concern for others. Do not let fear of what others might think of you limit the Spirit's work in your life. The Spirit works to connect you with others. Feel the Spirit's gentle push.

Since we live by the Spirit, let us keep in step with the Spirit. Galatians 5:25

Spiritual Renewal

Help me to feel the joy of abiding in You.

YOUR WAITING BEFORE Me will always be rewarded with spiritual renewal. Though you often cannot see My plan worked out on a daily basis, trust Me that all things are working together for your good and the good of those you love. Keep a reserve of secret joy in Me hidden, protected, and beyond the reach of all. Here with Me, you build your reservoir of joy and peace. To cut this time short depletes your reserve and leaves you spiritually vulnerable.

When the Lord restored the fortunes of Zion, we were like those who dreamed. Our mouths were filled with laughter, our tongues with songs of joy. Then it was said among the nations, "The Lord has done great things for them." Psalm 126:1–2

AUGUST 23 —

The Cure for Petty Fears

Thank you, Lord, for being the Rock where I can place my feet when I am low.

COMPLETE TRUST IN Me is the cure for the petty fears that rise to attack you throughout the day. Fears about your finances or worry that your life lacks purpose, fears that cause your heart to condemn you. Will you gain that perfect trust in Me that overcomes your fears? A carefree life is offered to all who will trust Me completely. This is the life of faith demonstrated by My servants of old. When temptations arise, the cure is to put your heart quickly at rest because of your trust in My power and love. Heaven can use you marvelously when you have a heart at rest. Be patient and trust that I am working in your life and in the lives of all those you love.

Have I not commanded you? Be strong and courageous. Do not be afraid; do not be discouraged, for the LORD your God will be with you wherever you go. Joshua 1:9

Handcrafted Work

Jesus, show me Your way.

WHEN YOU ARE uncertain about what to do, obey My will as you know it. However, My will for each of My loved ones is meant to be specific. I want to move them beyond general obedience to My written Word. I seek to provide handcrafted work for each of My disciples. This is the possibility that results from full surrender and a receptive spiritual ear. It is the Heaven-like life that so few find. This intimacy is available to all but underutilized. It is the restoration of man's individual walk with Me. Each soul is meant to be united with Me for daily guidance and supply. This is the excellent way.

For we are God's handiwork, created in Christ Jesus to do good works, which God prepared in advance for us to do. Ephesians 2:10

I Loved You First

Save me, Lord, and I will be saved. Rescue me and I will be rescued.

I LOVED YOU first. Our Father and I reached out to you first. Your task today is to understand the depth of My love for you. I forgive your crimes against My will quickly. Turn over your regrets to Me and focus on the present. I want My followers to be continuously hopeful. Pray for more comprehension of Me and My nature. I am the same yesterday, today, and forever— ever loving, always forgiving. I am always reaching out a hand to help, encourage, and save. The more you understand Me, the more emotionally healthy and complete you will be.

We love because he first loved us. 1 John 4:19

A Garden of Delights

Jesus, help me to have a heart at peace throughout the day.

MAKE MY PEACE personal and intimate. A well-kept garden is a restful place, nourishing the mind and spirit with its delights. Life with Me is like having an unseen garden inside you with waterfalls, comfortable chairs, cool breezes, and pleasant temperatures; it is full of flowers, songbirds, sunshine, and shade—a garden of delights that is safe and protected from all harm. Though you may travel near and far and your work for the day be diverse, all is well within you. Remind yourself of the personal peace I give you. Say, "All is well within me."

Peace I leave with you; my peace I give you. I do not give to you as the world gives. Do not let your hearts be troubled and do not be afraid. John 14:27

AUGUST 27 –

Invisible Beauty

Lord, thank You for this trip to Lake Michigan. Help me move beyond the mundane and see Your beauty.

SEEK BEAUTY. My beauty is all around you. It is in clear waters, gentle waves, vast horizon, gentle hillsides, and fruitful trees. Let your acknowledgement of My created beauty stir remembrance of the invisible beauty you have from the heavenly realm. This morning, take My gifts of full acceptance, unconditional love, and eternal life. The beauty in the world around you is inspiring; let it inspire thoughts of the greater spiritual rewards of the Christian life.

For every house is built by someone, but God is the builder of everything. Hebrews 3:4

I Fill You with Love

Jesus, grant me renewal. Refresh me as only You can.

HERE IN THIS quiet place, I can bestow My love upon you. A full dose from Me can carry you through this day. Here, there can be a transference of what you need the most. I fill you with love. With this love, you can overcome all. Love conquers all that presses against you, all that would rob you of joy. Say today, "I am full of His love."

And to know this love that surpasses knowledge—that you may be filled to the measure of all the fullness of God. Ephesians 3:19

Complete Surrender

Lord, thank You for this day. Help me rise above petty irritations and find Your abundant life.

FOCUS TODAY ON surrendering every blessing, trial, weakness, strength, frustration, joy, and want to Me. Share all with Me. During your day say, "I surrender all to Him." Give Me each frustration and find solace and direction from Me. Share each problem with Me, and you will find a solution in Me. Pass along each grateful thought, and I will add to your joy. Tell Me of your trust in Me in each situation, and you will see that I add to your faith. Find your victory in complete surrender to Me.

Surrender your heart to God, turn to him in prayer, and give up your sins—even those you do in secret. Job 11:13–14 CEV

A Wonderful Unfolding

Lord, piece me back together as only You can.

I KNOW YOU feel lowly and defeated. Wait on Me. I will provide other opportunities. Just listen to what I whisper to your heart. Simply wait with a smile, full of great expectation. Wait with a heart full of hope. You were created in God's image with unique traits and capabilities that were designed in the heavenly realm. However, to obtain your Jesus-infused personality, you must take all that you are—your heart, mind, and will—and surrender them to the Lord of lords. I am able to draw out the nectar of all that you were meant to be. I am able to make the rough edges of your personality smooth. A wonderful unfolding will occur, piece by piece, day by day.

God, pick up the pieces. Put me back together again. You are my praise! Jeremiah 17:14 MSG

AUGUST 31 –
Enlarge Your Joy

Jesus, You are my solution for all of life's problems. Be big in my life today.

I AM IN the still small voice that speaks to the needs of your heart. My voice may be subtle and mild, but that is My way. Today, acknowledge the truth that in this world you will have trouble. It is your spiritual task to keep My peace in the midst of distress. Say today, "No matter what, I'm going to Heaven." Let no trouble in this life take from you the peace that the promise of eternal life provides. You will have Heaven forever and foretastes of Heaven here in this life as well. Let this focus on eternity enlarge your joy and shrink your worries.

My sheep listen to my voice; I know them, and they follow me. John 10:27

True Peace of Mind

Lord, I give to You my discouragement. I know that time spent in Your presence will right all.

MAN SO OFTEN fails to find the peace of mind he seeks. He sees hints of it here and there. He may find a touch of it for himself on a golf course, at a football game, or while fishing. But these are shadows of the real peace found only in Me. Sit here, soak in a heavenly atmosphere, and you are renewed. True peace of mind is what your quiet time with Me means for your soul. Rest and true peace are provided to you in large measure. Soak them in.

The Lord is close to the brokenhearted and saves those who are crushed in spirit. Psalm 34:18

Love from Above

*Jesus, thank You for Your deposit of peace this morning
and the gift of sanity and order in a troubled world.*

IN THE BEGINNING, darkness and disorder reigned
in the universe. Surrounded by God in tri-part, the
earth was formed. The same is true for each person
who turns to God. Surrounded by love from above,
he is transformed. Confusion is turned to clarity. The
ruffled becomes unruffled. Uncertainty is replaced with
certainty. Mere existence is exchanged for true life. I
have placed you where I want you to be. Move beyond
your lack of faith and conquer with the faith you have.
The God who created the Heavens and the earth can
remove obstacles and make your path straight.

Now the earth was formless and empty, darkness was
over the surface of the deep, and the Spirit of God was
hovering over the waters. Genesis 1:2

Joy and Assurance

Jesus, grant me the joy that can only come from You. Direct my paths and give me the courage to obey You in all things.

BE CONFIDENT THAT I am setting you aside for increased work for Me. It is a heavenly-assured you that I need for the Father's work. Build up others with the confidence that it is from Me, your Lord, who stirs your actions. Work in the calm assurance that I labor beside you, blessing what you do. Joy and assurance are yours as you wait with Me. Today say to yourself, "I have joy and assurance from Jesus."

And the work of righteousness shall be peace; and the effect of righteousness, quietness and assurance forever. Isaiah 32:17 NKJV

Stand Firm

Lord, perform Your soul surgery this morning. Change my heart. Lift my downcast spirit.

A NEW DAY I give you. A lot can happen in a day. Stock markets can rise and fall. Business deals are won or lost. And a discouraged Christian can find new courage in Me. Your path today? Hold on. Stand firm. Sometimes it is enough to stand. Be firm in your belief that better days lie ahead and that other doors will open for you. Lift your head and look to Me. One look and you are changed. I am the solid Rock on which you stand.

Be on your guard; stand firm in the faith; be courageous; be strong. 1 Corinthians 16:13

SEPTEMBER 5 –
I Am with You

*I thank You, Jesus, for the relationship I have with You
that I can take with me throughout the day.*

THE LIGHT OF My presence brightens your path. It is your strength, hope, and the key to success. Consider my servants of old—Joseph, Daniel, David—their success was rooted in living their lives in God's presence. I am the source of all joy. The more you are aware of My presence, the greater your joy will be and the more influence you can have for the kingdom. Bring Me into every moment. Say to yourself, "Jesus is with me all day."

Potiphar noticed this and realized that the LORD was with Joseph, giving him success in everything he did. Genesis 39:3 NLT

A Beautiful Life

Whatever I have, Lord, help me to use it to the full for You.

YOUR MEASURE OF success is the amount of My will others see put in place in your life. Even the world sees the beauty of a life lived for what a person is best suited. The godless musician's lifework may bring pleasure to many fans. The unbelieving baseball coach may serve as a mentor to countless players. But no soul can be as beautiful as the one who aligns itself with Heaven's aims. No soul can have the simple majesty of one carefully crafted by Heaven's hand. Serve Me in the little and large things, and together we will build a beautiful life. A life of living well. A light to a dark world. A soft note in a cacophony of noise. A smile in a room full of unhappy people.

For those God foreknew he also predestined to be conformed to the image of his Son, that he might be the firstborn among many brothers and sisters. Romans 8:29

SEPTEMBER 7 –
Childlike Needs

*Thank you, Father and Jesus, for being true and faithful
to me even when my hope is low and my faith lacking.*

CHILDLIKE NEEDS ARE always the *real* needs, hidden and covered by layers of barriers. Man hides the things his soul craves in a fierce manner. Man's need is to be deeply loved by his heavenly Father and to feel His approval. Let Me show you the way. Consider how Our Father expressed His love for Me when I was on the earth. See the importance of His words spoken at My baptism in the Jordon River and My transfiguration on the Galilean mountainside. If I was encouraged by these words, how much more do My followers need to be reminded of the Father's love and acceptance? There is no substitute for these times away from your daily tasks and worries. Say today, "My Father loves me and is proud of me."

And a voice from heaven said, "This is my Son, whom I love; with him I am well pleased." Matthew 3:17

Breadcrumbs

Jesus, deliver me from fear and failure.

I ALWAYS LEAVE My breadcrumbs for you to find your way back. The forest is dark and cold; little light enters there. But nearby is the green meadow, a restful glade with pleasant sunshine. Turn with Me and leave the forest. Leave evil behind to rot in the dark. Step with Me on the pathway that leads to Heaven's love and grace, where all things are made new.

By day the pillar of cloud did not fail to guide them on their path, nor the pillar of fire by night to shine on the way they were to take. Nehemiah 9:19

The Waiting Time

Lord, let me be in the bubble of Your presence. Also, give me joyful work for You.

PERFECT PEACE I long to give My followers, My dear ones. The waiting time with Me is necessary. Few follow the good advice to be still and know that I am God. The waiting time allows you to experience Me. It allows you to have more than mere belief in Me; it allows you to know Me. Here in your secret place with Me, you can absorb the choice gifts Heaven has to offer: inner peace and definite guidance. Say, "I have perfect peace."

He says, "Be still, and know that I am God." Psalm 46:10

SEPTEMBER 10 –

Begin Again

Jesus, thank You for fall weather and the beauty in the turning leaves. Let me find myself in You again today.

BEGIN AGAIN TODAY. This is ever the Christian's call day to day. When your worldly conditions are rough and when they are smooth, begin again each day with Me. Live with Me and you have My peace in your inner core. This is the peace within I long for all My followers to obtain each morning. Go slowly today without the haste that mars many of My witnesses. Go with the faith that I have the power to change all. Live to provide hope to others that they, too, may begin again today and every day.

Praise be to the God and Father of our Lord Jesus Christ! In his great mercy he has given us new birth into a living hope through the resurrection of Jesus Christ from the dead, and into an inheritance that can never perish, spoil or fade. 1 Peter 1:3–4

The Christian Life

Let me find Your good gifts in full measure.

DELVE INTO THAT garden that is within you. Rest in that internal quiet meadow with bubbling brook, soft moss, and rays of sunshine. Truly, all is well when you turn to Me and to the quiet refuge hidden within you. Joy you will have in Heaven, but there is joy for you now with Me. The Christian life is more about being whole through contact with Me than in doing things for Me. Rest here with Me before you move out into the world.

The Lord will guide you always; he will satisfy your needs in a sun-scorched land and will strengthen your frame. You will be like a well-watered garden, like a spring whose waters never fail. Isaiah 58:11

SEPTEMBER 12 –
The Wonder of the Benevolence

Jesus, thank You for allowing me to come into Your presence. Grant me the self-discipline to give thanks to You in all circumstances.

GRAY DAYS ARE days for gratitude. Thank Me for your faith and health. Thank Me for your wife, children, parents, and Kentucky home. Thank Me for the supply I provide you. Thank Me for your friends, church, and for useful work for Me. Thank Me for the many blessings you have in the spiritual world, salvation, and the fruit of the Spirit. Thank Me until you feel the wonder of the benevolence Heaven has bestowed on your life. See in this how Heaven has adopted you as its son.

See what great love the Father has lavished on us, that we should be called children of God! And that is what we are! 1 John 3:1

The Gift of a New Heart

Lord, grant me a new heart this morning. Repair those parts I have damaged and those the world has scarred.

LET MY LOVE penetrate your heart—softening here, cleansing there. The miracle power of being a believer rests in the access each soul has to the power to rejuvenate his inner being. Where else does that power reside? In these quiet moments, the dark places of your heart are healed, the weak parts are strengthened, and the scarred parts are made new. I, your Great Physician, still work My miracles. I give you the gift of a new heart.

Cleanse me with hyssop, and I will be clean; wash me, and I will be whiter than snow . . . Create in me a pure heart, O God, and renew a steadfast spirit within me. Psalm 51:7, 10

SEPTEMBER 14 –
Little Courtesies

Jesus, show me how I can put the kingdom first today.

THE KINGDOM OFTEN advances silently and frequently through little courtesies. Small signs of love and kindness are darts to the chest of the evil one who wants a cruel, dark world. Change your world by acts of kindness. Seek to insert My Christianity into the world by gentleness and simple concern for others. Often the small acts matter most. A few gentle words may be more influential than a refined speech.

Because of the increase of wickedness, the love of most will grow cold, but the one who stands firm to the end will be saved. Matthew 24:12–13

Seasons of Joy

Thank You for the extra peace I feel this morning.

EMBRACE WHAT I give you this season. I remind you to be of good cheer when you have trouble, but I also plan seasons of joy and pleasant time on mountain slopes. Turn your back on Satan's weapons against you: doubt, fear, and the failure sense. I give you this season of full supply, joyous work, and family warmth. I give you times of refreshing. This season for you is like a boat ride on smooth water.

And those the Lord has rescued will return. They will enter Zion with singing; everlasting joy will crown their heads. Gladness and joy will overtake them, and sorrow and sighing will flee away. Isaiah 35:10

Respond with Love and Kindness

Jesus, give me wisdom to cope with the decisions of others.

IN EACH SITUATION, wait for instructions from Me. There is no rush to My plans. Peace for you flows from Heaven, where there is an eternity of peace. Be calm and unmoved despite the stress and strain surrounding you. Do not answer in-kind those who shout at you with the world's noise. Respond with love and kindness. By this, all men will know that you follow Me. Take self and personal feelings out of the picture, and you will see clearly. Feel deeply My eternal love for you, and you need less from others. You are empowered today to give, give, and give.

A gentle answer turns away wrath, but a harsh word stirs up anger. Proverbs 15:1

God Bids Me to Rest

Lord, I surrender my fatigue to You.

HERE ALONE WITH Me—outside in the early dawn—I can grant restoration for your soul. I will work on your behalf in the meantime. Rest in peace as your Master works for you. As you rest with Me, I can literally accomplish more than you would if you concentrated on your problems. You need more sleep. Go back to bed. Demonstrate your trust in Me by getting more sleep. Say today, "God bids me to rest."

In vain you rise early and stay up late, toiling for food to eat—for he grants sleep to those he loves.
Psalm 127:2

Enjoy Me as Your Great Friend

Jesus, through the grace that You provide, I have access to Your presence.

LET YOUR ENJOYMENT of being with Me and knowing Me be your high calling. Say today, "I enjoy Jesus." This demonstrates that you know who you are and what brings you true joy. It shakes the religious from your worship of Me. It speaks of a genuine faith of one of My followers. Keep Me as your Lord, Master, and King, but also enjoy Me as your great Friend.

I no longer call you servants, because a servant does not know his master's business. Instead, I have called you friends, for everything that I learned from my Father I have made known to you. John 15:15

SEPTEMBER 19 —
Thoughts of My Protection

Help me to enter into Your secret place.

STAY HERE WITH Me until your spirit is revived. Safety is the feeling of protection from danger. I keep you safe. It is one of My responsibilities as your Lord. As you allow this truth to sink in, your heart is encouraged. Your very countenance softens, and you are more pleasant to be around. Think thoughts of My protection and your guard drops, allowing you to encourage others more readily. Say, "I am kept safe by Him."

Keep me safe, my God, for in you I take refuge. Psalm 16:1

The Power of Acceptance

Jesus, help me see the good in others and myself today.

LEARN THE POWER of My acceptance, and you can change the world. Beneath the veneer of man lies fear, anxiety, and shame. Only Heaven's grace and acceptance remove these forces of evil. Here in your alone time with Me, you feel the Father's embrace and are restored. Your image is repaired. Your worth is rediscovered. Say today, "I have His full acceptance." Let this truth transform you as you live among so many who feel unaffirmed and rejected.

Instead of your shame you will receive a double portion, and instead of disgrace you will rejoice in your inheritance. Isaiah 61:7

My Workmanship

Lord, bring Your newness to this day. Make it fresh through Your power and grace.

LEXINGTON HORSE FARMS are known for their white wooden fences. Without continued maintenance, the boards rot. Without recoating with fresh paint, they become dull and brown. As you sit with Me each morning, you allow Me to recoat your life with grace and peace, making it an example of My workmanship for the world to see. Say today, "He coats me with grace and peace." This morning time is always available to you. I can take the dull and make it bright again.

For we are his workmanship, created in Christ Jesus for good works, which God prepared beforehand, that we should walk in them. Ephesians 2:10 ESV

The Path You Are to Walk

Lord, thank You for providing what I need in each situation. Lead me as You will.

MY WORK IN each life is unique. Just as no sunset is the same, the beauty of My work in each soul is specific for that person. To each, I lead as that person needs, as their internal disposition, strengths, and weaknesses require. And so with you. The quiet man is pushed into busy circles of activity. Through your marriage, four children, church, business, and law practice, the life I plan for you stretches you and requires your reliance on Me. Each pressure on your life is provided to build you up, not tear you down. Each leading takes you on the path you are to walk with Me.

In their hearts humans plan their course, but the LORD establishes their steps. Proverbs 16:9

His Full Supply

Jesus, I face today knowing that You will supply all I need.

OBEY ME IN all things, and the joy you seek will follow. The coordinated plans of My kingdom require the steadfast obedience of My servants. Little errands here. A word of encouragement to give there. A lifestyle change at times. A new location sometimes. You are on the right path, and I will supply all you need. Say today, "I have His full supply." Believe that I have full power to supply all your needs, material and spiritual. See My supply as a waterfall on a rushing river with limitless water, more upon more. All is given to you at the right time according to My will for you.

And my God will meet all your needs according to the riches of his glory in Christ Jesus. Philippians 4:19

Your Christian Aim

Jesus, I seek Your presence and Your will for my life today.

GIVE LITTLE SIGNS of love wherever you go, and you give Me to the world. Let your soul sense My loving pressure here and there throughout your day. Let My Spirit permeate to the depths of your inner being. Do not focus on having a manly nature. Make it your Christian aim to be a loving man, remade daily by heavenly resources. Nothing is stronger than love. Let My grace wash away sin and make you whole. Let your goal today to be a loving man to all you meet.

The goal of this command is love, which comes from a pure heart and a good conscience and a sincere faith. 1 Timothy 1:5

The Joy of the Simple Christian Life

Jesus, I understand so little, but You understand all. Lead me past my frustrations to Your peace and calm.

KNOW THE FULL joy of the simple Christian Life, the childlike life of one who trusts and accepts gladly. Rid yourself of all preconceived notions of entitlement: who you think you should be and what you think you should have. Surrender this day, week, season to Me, and your life will feel complete. Be content with knowing Me. Be content with My plans for your life. Say today, "Jesus, have Your way."

Blessed are the pure in heart, for they will see God. Matthew 5:8

The Joy of Living in the Middle of Each Day

Lord, thank You for a refreshing night's sleep and more energy today.

THIS DAY IS bright, clean, and untarnished. See this day as unmarred by past regrets or future worries. Use your faith in My saving grace to rid yourself of guilt from yesterday. Use your trust in My protection to shield you from tomorrow's worries. Strive to see each moment of this day separately, as a different gift from Me. It is a rich skill for the Christian to have the joy of living in the middle of each day in the company of his Savior. Say today, "Jesus, I want to live this moment with You."

A new day will dawn on us from above because our God is loving and merciful. Luke 1:78 GW

Count Your Blessings

Jesus, help me focus on what is good and all that I should be thankful for.

GRUMBLING IS A form of godlessness. Coach your mind by telling it what to think. Counting your blessings is not a quaint platitude from your elders. It is a self-discipline that sets My followers apart from the world. When you do not feel blessed is the best time to thank Me. Say thank you all the time as your recognition of what I have done and am doing in your life. Say thank you for what I am doing in the lives of your loved ones. Say today, "Lord, thank you for …" and let causes of gratefulness spring from your heart. Pray grateful prayers until your heart changes.

Do everything without grumbling or arguing, so that you may become blameless and pure children of God without fault in a warped and crooked generation.
Philippians 2:14–15

SEPTEMBER 28 —
Jesus Is with Me

Lord, help me make sense of all that has happened in the last twelve hours.

DO NOT GO at life alone today. Make yourself aware of My presence. Say, "I am not alone; Jesus is with me." Let this give you the thing you need the most—courage for the day. With courage comes hope because I am not only with you, but working on your behalf. Take captive each thought. Press upon your mind the fact that I am with you. In turn, I will provide you with peace of mind you would not think possible.

And the peace of God, which transcends all understanding will guard your hearts and your minds in Christ Jesus. Philippians 4:7

Master of Wind and Waves

Lord, my strength comes from You. I look to You for all hope and peace.

YOU CAN KEEP peace in your heart regardless of your circumstances. Say to the world around you as I did to the wind and waves in the boat, "Peace! Be still!" In doing so, you do not make a plea for peace, but you draw on Heaven's might to command peace to come to you. In this way, Heaven's foes, chaos and calamity, shrink back in fear. Peace! Be still! I am still the Master of the wind and waves around you. You can always have My perfect peace.

The LORD gives strength to his people; the LORD blesses his people with peace. Psalm 29:11

SEPTEMBER 30 –
Jesus Lives in Me

Jesus, renew me from within as only You can.

LET ME BE your source of confidence. Say today, "Jesus lives in me." Let this put you on the spiritual offensive and take you off spiritual defense. Let this be what calls out to your dry bones to come alive. Let this breathe life to the deadened parts of your soul. Let this spark joyful thoughts in your dulled mind. Let this draw hope from a heart that has hardened. Say, "Jesus lives in me."

Examine yourselves to see whether you are in the faith; test yourselves. Do you not realize that Christ Jesus is in you? 2 Corinthians 13:5

Goodness from Above

Lord, thank You for Your goodness to me.

YOUR INNATE SENSE of what is good comes from Our Father and the realm of Heaven, where goodness reigns. Our Father is good. Providing good to others is simply an extension of what it means to be a Christ-follower. Say, "I have His goodness" as a reminder of the gift I give you through the Spirit. Let goodness be in your heart and shine forth on your face. In this dark world, you have goodness from above.

And do not forget to do good and share with others, for with such sacrifices God is pleased. Hebrews 13:16

Come Away, Alone with Me

Jesus, thank You that I can meet with You each day.

COME AWAY, ALONE with Me, your ever-present helper. Alone with Me, you find strength and encouragement. Here with Me, you find supply for your daily needs. Alone, you remember that your real treasure is secured for you in eternity. Alone, you are able to sort out the important from the unimportant. Alone, you find Me, your great reward.

After this, the word of the LORD came to Abram in a vision: "Do not be afraid, Abram. I am your shield, your very great reward." Genesis 15:1

Your Work Is to Call Everyone Home

Lord, help me to see the world as You would have me see it. Put my heart in the right place.

IT IS A hurting world we are out to save—one soul at a time. This is your lifework. All else matters so little. With your acknowledgement of My power and authority, you are able to join Me in healing the sick all around you. Soul starvation is rampant. Separation anxiety from our good Father is widespread. Partner with Me to help others make sense out of their lives. Remind some of My followers of the faith they have in Me. Tell others of the hope of Heaven they can possess. Your work is to call everyone home.

Instead, they were longing for a better country—a heavenly one. Hebrews 11:16

Jesus Is Living Water for Me

Jesus, give life its meaning today. Grant me certainty when I feel uncertain.

LAND WITHOUT WATER is a desert. A person without water is dehydrated. A soul without living water is desperate. Let My living water flow through you, replenishing your soul. Picture My living water bubbling forth from your heart, cleansing you, making you whole. See around you the desperate trying to find satisfaction in life without Me. My living water fills your soul with all good things. Let it flow from you today to bless the lives of others. Help the desperate to see that they really thirst for Me. Tell them that you, too, are desperate without Me. Say today, "Jesus is living water for me."

Jesus answered, "Everyone who drinks this water will be thirsty again, but whoever drinks the water I give them will never thirst. Indeed, the water I give them will become in them a spring of water welling up to eternal life." John 4:13–14

Know Your Seasons

Lord, I am weary. Give me a receptive ear to hear the Spirit's call today. Give me a soft heart to sense Your will.

TEMPERATURES DROP AS the earth ebbs from the sun. Squirrels prepare by storing away their secret stash of acorns. Bears add layers of fat for warmth and nourishment. Birds fly to a warmer climate for easier living. You should know your seasons too. The busy man adds silence to his schedule for his return to sanity. You should search for a place to rest. You need a quiet day, some hours of quiet repose. Let quietness be a dear friend today. In quietness, you will find Me and the solace your soul craves. Say today, "Quietness with Him makes me whole."

There is a time for everything, and a season for every activity under the heavens. Ecclesiastes 3:1

Life Is Meant to Be Lived in Jesus' Presence

Good morning, Lord. Please bring me back in sync with You.

RUSH AND WORRY block you from sensing My nearness. Count all else as loss in comparison with sensing My presence. It is always a Spirit of love that greets you when you are aware of Me. You are grounded when you act out of this awareness. So often man's actions are motivated by his needs or desires. The Christian connected to Me acts out of his completeness. The one abiding in Me is motivated from his sense of wholeness. Say to yourself, "Life is meant to be lived in Jesus' presence." Go in My peace.

My heart says of you, "Seek his face!" Your face, LORD, I will seek. Psalm 27:8

A Full Dose of Eternal Life

Jesus, thank You for Your rich mercy and the life it provides.

IN YOUR HIDING place here, I give you a full dose of eternal life. Let it pass through your veins until you are changed. It is like oxygen-rich blood that returns your soul to health. Eternal life provides a spirit of grace that animates My believers. It is the blessing from Calvary and the protection from Golgotha. It is the joy of the saved.

Jesus said to her, "I am the resurrection and the life. The one who believes in me will live, even though they die." John 11:25

A Scarred Life

Jesus, protect me from a generational spirit of pride and false manhood. Influence me with Your authentic manhood so that I can pass it on to others.

AN AUTHENTIC MAN is a man who is in the spiritual battle. He is not the man who denies there are battles that rage within him. He is not the man who seeks to conquer through his own power. He is not the man who hides from conflicts at home or in his relationships. He is the man who knows victory is gained through surrender to a loving Savior. From times like these—of quiet communion—you go out with the power to bless and help. A scarred life helping another scarred life. A broken man reaching out to help another broken man. Christianity is a for-sinners-only religion. There is always hope in Me, first for yourself, then for those around you. Your life and the lives of those dear to you are tucked safely away with Me. Contact with Heaven is the cure for all of earth's ills.

For you know that it was not with perishable things such as silver or gold that you were redeemed from the empty way of life handed down to you from your ancestors, but with the precious blood of Christ, a lamb without blemish or defect. 1 Peter 1:18–19

OCTOBER 9 –

Greatness in Service

Let me hit the mark with my life, not as I will, but as You will.

THERE IS GREATNESS in service for Me. Personal fulfillment results from the discovery of the specific service intended for each of My disciples. It was divine fulfillment for the dreamer Joseph to save a nation, the boy David to face Goliath, the restored Peter to deliver the keys of salvation, the wise Stephen to face the hostile crowd, the remarkable Paul to answer the critics, and the lovable John to pen his letters. There is great joy in being the right tool in the Master's hand, working at the correct task. Seek daily to serve Me as Heaven has intended. Then your success will come as naturally as light from a burning candle.

Instead, whoever wants to be great among you must be your servant. Matthew 20:26

A Quiet Mind Rested in Me

Lord, I am weary. Help me filter all voices today except Yours.

RELAX IN MY love and care. Let there be no rushing about like the pagans. My disciples have an opportunity to show their trust in Me by their rest. Fear, worry, and brokenness prompt so many of man's activities. Let Me make you whole, and then there will be nothing fitful in your actions. All will be sown in peace with a quiet mind rested in Me. I know the storms that rage outside you and within you. I am with You. I am available to tell the wind and waves, "Quiet! Be still!" Rest in the certainty of My presence and power.

Jesus was in the stern, sleeping on a cushion. The disciples woke him and said to him, "Teacher, don't you care if we drown?" Mark 4:38

OCTOBER 11 –
Soul Building

Lord, I come to You once again and ask You to perform a miracle in my heart.

REMEMBER MY PARABLE about the house built on a rock. The home is secure even when the storm comes, and the wind blows violently against roof and shutter. You have spent your adult life soul building, imperfectly but earnestly. I will reward that, but the reward is in part already here. The foundation of your soul is firm and strong. Your daily emotions, which are not as deep, may wax and wane like shutters loosed by the storm. But as the storm dies down and the rain clouds pass, the sunlight will return. My lesson to you is do not worry about the broken shutters in the midst of the storm. They can be repaired. Your emotions may rage, but find joy that your inner self rests securely, even happily, with Me. Say today, "The real me rests with Jesus."

Therefore we do not lose heart. Though outwardly we are wasting away, yet inwardly we are being renewed day by day. 2 Corinthians 4:16

He Is in All My Details

Jesus, I believe in You more than my fears.

I BRING YOU times of refreshing like a cool breeze on a hot day. Step into today excited by what I have planned for you. The Christian life is a responsive one. I am the architect, and I design all the plans for you. Your responsibility is to build according to that master plan made known to you each day. Leave room in the details of your day for My sovereignty and new work orders. Greet each situation with a smile rooted in faith in Me and a firm hope that I am working in you and for you. Say today, "He is in all my details."

He is before all things, and in him all things hold together. Colossians 1:17

OCTOBER 13 —

Let Love Prompt All

Lord, pour out Your blessings on all those dear to me.

LOVE IS ALWAYS the secret weapon. I poured out love while on the earth. It is what exploded from the cross on Calvary. Accept My gifts of love and mercy. Accept these in full measure in order to be the loving man I wish you to be. Say today, "Let love prompt all I do and say." Put this on your heart, and I cannot help but use you.

Therefore love is the fulfillment of the law. Romans 13:10

Reflect My Light

Jesus, fix all the broken pieces in me so that I may serve You and pass Your encouragement on to others. Let my mark be Your mark.

MY PLANS MAY be simple, but Heaven's glory unfolds when you follow them. When your eyes are on Me, desiring to serve the kingdom, I can draw out what is best in you. I can do more than that; I can supply you with the gifts of the Spirit, so you have a reserve of love, joy, and peace to share with others. Remember that your path has been no mistake and no product of randomness. I can use all your life experiences to influence others. I want to use you to reflect My light in what is often a dark world. I give My grace for your past, My joy for your present, and My plans for a fruitful tomorrow.

No one lights a lamp and hides it in a clay jar or puts it under a bed. Instead, they put it on a stand, so that those who come in can see the light. Luke 8:16

Room for You at My Table

Please meet me here this morning. Encourage me with Your presence and plans.

I COME TO you; know that I always come. No power on earth could prevent Me from revealing Myself to you. No plan of man or scheme of the evil one could even slow My appearance in your life. I give you renewal this day as every day. There is always room for you at My table. Stay with Me as long as you want. You are always welcomed here.

When one of those at the table with him heard this, he said to Jesus, "Blessed is the one who will eat at the feast in the kingdom of God." Luke 14:15

Live Only in the Present

Thank You for the incredible rich colors I see all around me this morning.

THE BIRDS SING their happy song. Like you, they do not know what lies ahead. They only know that a new and beautiful day is before them. Yesterday's regrets or tomorrow's worries do not drag them down. You could fully enjoy the gifts I have given you if you would live only in the present. This is one of your weaknesses and often prevents you from enjoying what I give you moment to moment, day to day. Live this day with Me at the center of your life.

Forget the former things; do not dwell on the past. See I am doing a new thing! Now it springs up; do you not perceive it? I am making a way in the wilderness and streams in the wasteland. Isaiah 43:18–19

Sit with Me until My Message Is Clear

Lord, let me hear Your message for me today.

SIT WITH ME long enough so that glimmers of My thoughts turn into clear messages. Sit long enough until I reveal My thought for the day to you. Say, "My soul is satisfied with Jesus." Let this message be a reminder that I am the solution to all your problems and the supply for your deepest needs. Let it also fill you with joy because you have happily found Me. This is good news for all. Share with others how I give you personal hope and joy today. Sit with Me until My message is clear.

Guide me in your truth and teach me, for you are God my Savior, and my hope is in you all day long.
Psalm 25:5

My Command is to Wait

Help me make sense of my world and clarify my place in it.

YOU FEEL EMPTY because I have not placed you in a specific ministry for kingdom work. However, I have placed you where I want you. Put your doubts and insecurities aside. Your spiritual success results from hearing My will and obeying it. The results are in My realm and governance. In the life of every disciple, there are times of searching and yearning when My command is to wait. Do not feel lost in this season, but keep your identity fixed in Me. Plus, I have other work for you to do along the way. Do not worry or fret. The key is to want each of your steps to be blessed by Me. Say to yourself today, "Let every step be His step for me."

Therefore, holy brothers and sisters, who share in the heavenly calling, fix your thoughts on Jesus, whom we acknowledge as our apostle and high priest. Hebrews 3:1

OCTOBER 19 –

Your Heavenly Calling

Lord, I need a miracle in my heart today. Lift me out of this sense of gloom and depression.

SAY YOUR THANK-YOUS. This is your heavenly calling today. This discipline, when practiced and firmly adhered to, is a helpful tool to clear your sight and cleanse your heart. Be rigid in telling your mind what to think, and soon your feelings will follow. I have led you to your current path. You are on the right road. Stay with Me and wait patiently for My next steps for you. Thank Me for all, and I will lift from you the bad spirits that seek to weigh you down.

Take delight in the LORD, and he will give you the desires of your heart. Psalm 37:4

I Bind Your Wounds

Fill my spiritual tank today. I surrender my broken-ness to You. I see others who had a healthier spiritual upbringing, and I can be jealous. Help me first, and I will be available to help others.

I HAVE DONE much in your inner being to heal you, but some hurts you must continue to bring to Me. You envy another's close relationship with his dad. There is a lot you respect about your dad—honor that. Give full forgiveness for the balance as I have freely forgiven you. Do not imitate the unmerciful servant. Your sins against Heaven have been greater. Here you are granted full forgiveness, and I will give you even more. You know that I will sustain you and heal you. I bind your wounds. Receive what you need from Me today and every day. Then, turn to your hurting world and seek to be a beacon of light and hope. Your life is rich, and I will make it even richer.

He heals the brokenhearted and binds up their wounds.
Psalm 147:3

Jesus Makes Me Whole

Lord, thank You for Your presence here on the earth and in my life.

TIME WITH ME is like sitting by a clear mountain lake. It is pure and wholesome, beautiful and peaceful. Come back here sooner. You tarried too long without abiding in Me. You can accomplish little and cause disruption when you are out of sync with Me. Come back here, and I restore you to calm. Then, whole and at peace, you are a fit instrument to carry out My work. Say to yourself today, "Jesus makes me whole."

Then they cried out to the LORD in their trouble, and he brought them out of their distress. He stilled the storm to a whisper; the waves of the sea were hushed. Psalm 107:28–29

OCTOBER 22 –
Her Identity in Me

Lord, be with my daughter as she prepares to go back to college, where others will attempt to move her from her beliefs and identity in You.

TRUST IN ALL things, and the way will be made clear. Do not worry about her. She is where I would have her to be. Of all your children, she is most capable in this—capable of continuing in her identity in Me, but also capable of taking on a room full of scoffers and naysayers. I have instilled a spirit in her that does not shrink back. All is well. She will be kept safe and will be a light to others. Your joy is to sit back and say, "I could not be prouder."

But we do not belong to those who shrink back and are destroyed, but to those who have faith and are saved. Hebrews 10:39

OCTOBER 23 —
Joyful Service

Lord, help me move beyond my little world and be a man who sees the needs of others.

THE JOY-FILLED LIFE emerges as you learn to die to self. Dying to self is positive because it makes way for joyous kingdom work. I will fill your days with useful things. The tasks I give you are Heaven's errands, but they serve you too. Without them, you are lost in self: self-pity, self-desires, and self-preoccupation. In the kingdom—both now and for all eternity—you will have joyful service, service that brings pieces of Heaven to others and joy to yourself. It is not My children who lack the joy of life, but those enwrapped in their own selfish pursuits and inward thinking. Serve Me by helping those I put on your path. Then the clouds part, and My sunshine breaks forth on your day. Say to yourself, "Less about me, more about others."

Therefore, since we are surrounded by such a great cloud of witnesses, let us throw off everything that hinders and the sin that so easily entangles. Hebrews 12:1

A Home Fashioned in Love

Lord, help me be the best father I can be to my son.
Show me where I can be more and do more in his life.

JUST AS YOU give Me thanks for his special placement in your home, I am thankful for the turnings to Me that would not have happened without his place in your life. I will watch over him and keep him. His path may not be the one you would have picked, but I will be with him each step of the way, even if he is unaware of My presence in his life for a time. You do not go with him into the day, but I do! I am planning for him and putting the right people and situations in his life. Your household's influence on him has not been without effect, as you fear. I bring into My followers' lives not only those they can best help, but also those who can best help them. It is not the picture-perfect postcard I seek to create in your home, but a home fashioned in love, full of the joy of overcoming, and marked by genuine lives replete with victories and stumbles. Through all, I build a depth of character in you and an honest spiritual walk that will aid others. Wait and see what I will do through him. The scars that I allow will be used to help others.

What, then, shall we say in response to these things? If God is for us, who can be against us? Romans 8:31

OCTOBER 25–
Natural Light

Jesus, thank You for the beauty of autumn.

LIVING WITHOUT TAPPING into the Spirit's power is like living on a cloudy day; the sun is shining above the clouds, but you do not benefit from its rays. Natural light lets you see the full spectrum of colors, all of earth's beautiful shades. Limited light shows only part and parcel. Seek the spiritual in your life first, and then all else will fall into place. Being led by My Spirit is like seeing with natural light; everything is clearer, brighter, and more beautiful. See beyond your doubts. Be Spirit-led in all things.

But for you who revere my name, the sun of righteousness will rise with healing in its rays. And you will go out and frolic like well-fed calves. Malachi 4:2

OCTOBER 26 —

Downstream Rowing

Jesus, sometimes I do not know what to pray for, but I ask that You allow me to sense Your nearness, return me to a greater peace of mind, and give me opportunities to serve You with joy.

VIEW YOUR DAYS as a man in a rowboat. Sometimes when serving Me, you travel upstream with considerable stress and strain. Other times I guide you downstream with greater ease and comfort. Both directions are needed for the kingdom and add different qualities to your character. My lesson for you today is that your time of continued upstream rowing is ending. Soon I will grant you the peace and joy of downstream travel with the wind at your back. You have served Me well through an extended period of trials; I now guide you to a period filled with greater sweetness and a more leisurely pace. As I remove obstacles in your path, I will provide rich spiritual opportunities for growing the kingdom: planting seeds, watering seeds, tending to young plants, and encouraging mature ones. Say today, "Lord, I'll take the downstream rowing."

He saw the disciples straining at the oars, because the wind was against them. Mark 6:48

OCTOBER 27 –

Heaven Loves a Celebration

Jesus, I cast all my worries on You. Free me to be light-hearted and have influence for You.

TODAY, FOLLOW ME, and do not let fear bar your way. Fear is the enemy and the enemy's tool is fear—fear of poverty, rejection, loneliness, and of leading a meaningless life. The remedy is simple. Replace fear and worry with trust and faith. Peace flows from a disciplined mind. When thoughts of worry run amok, the mind and spirit take a downward spiral. In this situation, and in every situation, remind yourself that all is well and that I can handle the details of your life in full. I provide your shield against the devil's arrows. Be of good cheer today. Heaven loves a celebration. Heaven celebrates when a sinner repents and turns back home. Heaven celebrates when its message falls on a responsive believer and is obeyed. Heaven celebrates when able-bodied men take up their cross and follow Me. Heaven celebrates when a believer turns away from worry and gains peace of mind through firm trust.

I tell you that in the same way there will be more rejoicing in heaven over one sinner who repents than over ninety-nine righteous persons who do not need to repent. Luke 15:7

A God Who Saves You and Stays with You

Lord, come save me, and I will be saved.

ONLY A STRONG God can save. Only a God who truly saves is relevant. Where can you find salvation except in Me? Where can you find renewal except in Me? Where can you find hope except in Me? I am with you to the end of the age. We have much to do together. Get back up today. Do not work alone, but invite Me to spend the day with you. I am the God who saves you and stays with you. This remaining makes all the difference. Have a genuine and deep abiding in Me.

Salvation is found in no one else, for there is no other name under heaven given to mankind by which we must be saved. Acts 4:12

Jesus Dwells in My Heart

Thank You, Lord, for the power of the sun that destroys darkness. Thank You for Your presence here that destroys evil within and without. Lead me as You would.

DISCIPLINE YOUR MIND today. It is the key to keeping your heart where you would have it to be. If you think thoughts of hope and grace, then your heart will be filled with those qualities. You have let your mind run free with negative and hurried thoughts. Say today, "Jesus dwells in my heart." Say this as a repellent to the forces of evil in the world and the enemy's darts and arrows. Say this as a triumphant call that helps you overcome the failure sense. Say this as a way of remembering that I forgive you completely of past mistakes. Say this to be sensitive to My hand guiding your day.

I pray that out of his glorious riches he may strengthen you with power through his Spirit in your inner being, so that Christ may dwell in your hearts through faith. Ephesians 3:16–17

OCTOBER 30 —
Use Me Always, Jesus

Thank you, Jesus, for this extended time to be with You. This makes all the difference.

THIS "VINE TIME" with Me changes all. Soak in My presence this morning. You feel unsettled and struggle to see your path to peace. Enjoy being in this atmosphere. Take peace from Me. Take joy from Me. I give these to you gladly. As always, you are changed by this time. Here I also give you strength for the day and tell you your next steps. Let your prayer today be, "Use me always, Jesus." I am putting other souls on your path for you to draw near to Me. You have asked for a life filled with imparting to others the things of Heaven, and that is what I am joyfully providing for you.

"Come, follow me," Jesus said, "and I will send you out to fish for people." Mark 1:17

Productive Days

Thank You, Jesus, that my life is not random and that You are a living and bright reality. I offer to You all the details of my day.

DISCOVER MY REVELATIONS in each part of your day by the power of substitution. Say today, "His choice here and now." This glad turning to Me, this continual search for My choice, will add much to your day. Let My will be substituted for your will in the big and small decisions of the day, moment to moment, hour by hour. And so, unrest will turn to rest, chaos to order, and fruitless hours to productive days. Find your way in this life by finding My way for you.

"For my thoughts are not your thoughts, neither are your ways my ways," declares the Lord. "As the heavens are higher than the earth, so are my ways higher than your ways and my thoughts than your thoughts." Isaiah 55:8–9

NOVEMBER 1 –
Adequate Rest

Lord, speak to me today despite my weariness.

THE LACK OF bounce in your step stems from your lack of discipline. Earlier to bed allows the Christian to rise, pray, and be prepared for the day. Your hour with Me should be early, but not forced again and again on a tired body that lacks adequate rest. I still send glad tidings to you this morning. Go in the strength you have. There is always sufficient grace for you.

The spirit is willing, but the flesh is weak. Matthew 26:41

Joy-Filled Nature

Lord, I want to pause this morning to praise You for the beauty I see all around me.

IMITATE NATURE'S HALLELUJAHS all around you. The golden hues of fall are brilliant. See the beauty in the dark yellow and rich red leaves. Joy-filled nature sings praises in chorus to its King. Let the joy of the Lord be your strength as well, a joy no person can take from you. Often let the beauty of My creation be the springboard that brings you to Heaven's gates.

Let the fields be jubilant, and everything in them; let all the trees of the forest sing for joy. Psalm 96:12

Heaven's Perfection

Lord, help me align my life with Your wishes for me.

OUR FATHER AND I are one. I have commanded you to be perfect as our Father in Heaven is perfect. Our Father's will reigns supreme in Heaven. Let His will rule in your heart today. When you make effort to align yourself with Heaven's will, then you perfect your life. This is true even if your attempts at perfection fall short. Make your best effort to follow His will and only His will. When yesterday's efforts are marred by imperfections, allow My rich grace to cover you. Rise and begin again today striving for Heaven's perfection.

Be perfect, therefore, as your heavenly Father is perfect. Matthew 5:48

Every Day a Revolution

Lord, thank You for Your many gifts to me. Help me to be a useful instrument for You. Cleanse me and make me pure. Give me ears to hear Your voice and eyes to see Your will.

EVERY DAY IS a revolutionary day for My followers. I stand and wait and receive so few—far too few—responses to My call for revolution. Respond today to My humble pleas. Your revolution for Me is to call others to freedom. Freedom from sin's tyranny and the devil's schemes. Freedom from the weight of selfish desires. Freedom for every soul to gain the God-designed personality it was designed to possess. Love Me by helping those I send your way. Know the joy of receiving and then doing God's will in an undivided life. Start a revolution in the lives of those I send to you.

It is for freedom that Christ has set us free. Stand firm, then, and do not let yourselves be burdened again by a yoke of slavery. Galatians 5:1

NOVEMBER 5 —
Daily Renewal

Thank You for spending this time with me today and every day.

YOU ARE RIGHT to come to Me to be refreshed. Here I provide you inward renewal day after day. This is how man was meant to live, each day absorbing new, life-giving energy and direction. This is your manna for an empty stomach, your cool water for a parched mouth. I provide you peace of mind that calms your fears and eliminates your angst. Let your quiet calm effect those you encounter today.

Even youths grow tired and weary and young men stumble and fall; but those who hope in the LORD will renew their strength. Isaiah 40:30–31

Travel Light

Lord, take away all that bothers me, all that saddens me.

YOUR SPIRITUAL LESSON is to carve out all that does not help the kingdom or further your role in it. Throw out all that hinders. Spiritual buoyancy comes from traveling light. Throw off guilt and shame, doubt and sin, and you keep your head above water. Stay long enough with Me to cast those on Me, and I will take them away. Say today, "I travel light with Jesus." It is the simple but meaningful faith of the straightforward man that changes the world.

Therefore, since we are surrounded by such a great cloud of witnesses, let us throw off everything that hinders and the sin that so easily entangles. Hebrew 12:1

Love Banishes Fear

Lord, let me see You and Your strength above the things that press down on me.

FEAR IS THE curse of the world. Man is afraid—afraid of poverty, loneliness, unemployment, sickness, and failure. Fear has no place in the kingdom. Love banishes fear, and trust fights off the evil spirit of worry. Let love and trust rule in your life today. Let your smile be a demonstration of My love's dominion in your heart. Say today, "Christ's love is stronger."

"I am the LORD your God who takes hold of your right hand and says to you, Do not fear; I will help you." Isaiah 41:13

Pass on to Others

Lord, put meaningful work in my life.

A SELFLESS LOVE is what I have provided to you and is what I am asking you to pass on to others. Love others more. Love yourself less. Discover where I am working and how you can join Me. Walk with Me today in My pursuit of others. Love Me more by loving those I put on your path. Say to yourself today, "He loves me with all His heart; I will pass His love on to others."

For Christ's love compels us, because we are convinced that one died for all, and therefore all died. 2 Corinthians 5:14

The Right Path

Show me Your path today.

PEACE AND ENERGY flow from grace and purity. Love and joy spring from a sense of belonging and useful work. Oh, the thrill for man to walk with Me and be in step with the Spirit. Undivided fellowship with your Master and friend demonstrates true discipleship; it is a love-based, not fear-based, relationship. You have much to learn from those who have lived by grace year after blessed year, but you are on the right path.

Whether you turn to the right or to the left, your ears will hear a voice behind you, saying, "This is the way; walk in it." Isaiah 30:21

NOVEMBER 10 –
To Rescue and Save

Thank you, Lord, for being strong to save.

I NEED MORE followers to sign up for service for Me. Life with Me is meant to be an adventure and not a sedentary lifestyle. A Coast Guard team has a powerful ship that is freshly painted and well-equipped with lifelines, life jackets, and life preservers. It stands ready to answer the call of one in distress. My brother, we serve together to rescue those lost and in despair with all of Heaven's equipment. Man has worked very hard to replace Me and fill his soul with that which does not lead to life. Come, we travel together to rescue and save.

Rescue those being led away to death. Proverbs 24:11

NOVEMBER 11 –

Personality Created by God

Lord, help me to love You with all my heart and mind.

LET THIS BE your refrain today: "I love the Lord with all my heart." Let it indicate your total surrender to Heaven's reign in your life. Let it mark your death to worldly self and pathway to revealing a personality created by God. Your true self is discovered when you love Me with all your heart. The surprise for man is that this devotion to Heaven makes his identity clear. Here he finds personal joy when I draw out the image of God hidden within him. And so with you. This is the real you that will help your fellow man. Love Me with all your heart.

Jesus replied, "Love the Lord your God with all your heart and with all your soul and with all your mind."
Matthew 22:37

Spiritual and Financial Health

Lord, my needs in all areas seem to outweigh my supply. Show me Your way.

YOU CRAVE SPIRITUAL and financial health. You know that I am your only source for each. You must take sufficient time to be with Me. Soaking in My presence is a need for man like no other. There is no substitute for sufficient time to absorb all that Heaven has to offer you. I will not let you fail. I will supply all your spiritual and material needs. Let your mind rest in My grace and a feeling of plenty will come to you. I will provide richly all you need.

Remain in me, as I also remain in you. No branch can bear fruit by itself; it must remain in the vine. Neither can you bear fruit unless you remain in me. John 15:4

Humility

Jesus, speak to me plainly. Let Your message be clear.

QUIETLY SERVE THE King of kings, Lord of lords. Go forth in faith, not having the answers, but knowing the One who does. This adds a humility to your character that is appealing to others. A show-off, a know-it-all, repels others and hinders the kingdom. A gentle, humble soul draws in others. Appeal to others with an honest humility, and in doing so, you will bring Heaven to earth.

But knowledge puffs up while love builds up.
1 Corinthians 8:1

Laughter and Continual Joy

Let me be the best man I can be today for my family.

BE THE LEADER your family needs. Deny yourself; serve them. Serve them by adding joy to your household. Where can you laugh together? Where can you add fun to their day? See your day as being lived out in My presence, where there is laughter and continual joy. Dear friend, you are being carefully guided and effectively used. Hear and obey My voice, and you can be a heavenly force on this earth. Focus today on your own family.

Our mouths were filled with laughter, our tongues with songs of joy. Psalm 126:2

NOVEMBER 15 —
Live Today for Me

Lord, I feel like a boat tossed about by strong waves with no way to move out of the storm and no rudder to steer away from danger. Give me Your words of life.

YOU ADD GREASE to the squeaking wheel. You apply ointment to the burn. Provide grace and love to your human frailties. Move past your hurt feelings and up and over the barriers to your joy. Take the focus off what causes you to struggle. Do not think about past mistakes. Surrender all the day's pressures to Me. Live today for Me. Today is where I am. I am always in your today. Say, "He gives me joy today."

The Lord has done it this very day; let us rejoice today and be glad. Psalm 118:24

NOVEMBER 16 –

Sweet Friendship

Thank You for the friends in my life.

A SWEET FRIENDSHIP is like continual fresh air. It is a gift to yourself to make your closest earthly connections with those who follow Me. To spend time with those who are daily refreshed by Me is to provide for yourself a bountiful garden bursting with good fruit. Conversely, to be closest with those who follow the way of the world is to invite ruin to your life. You need My followers; they need you. My sheep were intended to remain together in this way, encouraging, challenging, and spurring one another to love and good works.

Do not be misled: "Bad company corrupts good character." 1 Corinthians 15:33

Circles of Community

Thank You for the richness my family and friends bring to my life.

STAY CONNECTED WITH Me and others. Our Father's great desire is to connect with all people. He sent Me to earth to provide forgiveness for all and to re-establish connection with all. Create connections all around you: with your wife, kids, extended family, church, and community. So much that life has taught you needs to be untaught. Self-reliance and independent living are to be cast by the wayside as refuse and hauled away. In their place, I wish to bestow upon you a more meaningful manner of living—one with significant and impactful connections with others made possible only when you are connected with Me. Satan wishes to separate you from others. My wish is for you to live in circles of community.

All the believers were together and had everything in common. Acts 2:44

Fit Instrument

Jesus, thank You for a new start and the chance to bounce back.

YOU ARE RIGHT to start with Me each day, only so can I mold your heart and character. You change as you spend time alone with Me. Like Moses on the mountainside, you emerge from this time of communion sharpened, renewed, and reshaped, the creation made better by being with its Creator. Spending time with Me makes you a fit instrument for each of Heaven's callings and allows you the joy of doing My work.

In a large house there are articles not only of gold and silver, but also of wood and clay; some are for special purposes and some for common use. Those who cleanse themselves from the latter will be instruments for special purposes, made holy, useful to the Master and prepared to do any good work. 2 Timothy 2:20–21

Layer by Layer

Lord, show me Your will for me.

LAYER BY LAYER, My will is revealed to you. Your part is to rejoice along the way. Relax! Heaven is calling you each day. My lessons for you are simple: live each day with Me and allow Me to heal you and give you instructions. To know Me and to do My will, results in a joy that earth's aims cannot provide. Allow Me to feel the joy of your childlike trust. You only need to know Heaven's goals for this day.

Trust in the Lord with all your heart and lean not on your own understanding. Proverbs 3:5

Hearing and Obeying

Let me feel today that I am doing Your good in the world.

DOUBT IS A tool the evil one employs to kill hope and crush joy. Faith in Me protects you from this deadly tool. Faith is belief in a good result before it happens. Faith is belief in the sap that flows secretly beneath the bark in winter. Faith is belief in the bud when the flower is not yet ready to open. Faith is belief in the water nourishing the fruit tree whose season has not yet come. Faith is the man who obeys Me and trusts the results to Me. It is your duty to listen and obey. My plans are always formed in love. Trust the result to Me. Believe that My result will be a blessing for you and your corner of the world. True faith is shown by obedience when you do not know the result. Your success is hearing and obeying.

Now faith is confidence in what we hope for and assurance about what we do not see. Hebrews 11:1

Smile and Observe Others

Thank You for meeting with me today and every day.

TRUE CONNECTION WITH Me changes the heart. Quality time with Me keeps the heart soft and pure. There is a difference between a forced smile and one that emanates from a heart at peace. This is what it means to radiate Christ in your life. It is the quality of your life (or condition of your heart) that most affects others. Smile today from a heart that is hidden away with Me, protected from all evil, and guided toward all good. Smile and observe others. Only by observing others, by observing the condition of their hearts, can you hope to help them. You do not observe enough. Smile and observe, and then I will show you what to do and say.

I will instruct you and teach you in the way you should go; I will counsel you with my loving eye on you.
Psalm 32:8

Order to Your Life, Home, and Affairs

Manage me, Lord, for I cannot manage myself.

THIS STATEMENT IS true for all on the earth, but few realize it. Self-sufficiency and pride bar My entrance to man's heart. As you continue to seek My guidance for every area of your life, you show that you are willing to be humble. In turn, I can bring order to your life, home, and affairs. Whoever gives control of his life to Me, will find that I instill in him an ordered life, a life full of My peace and joy. I am a God of order, not disorder. In My feeding of the five thousand, there was no chaotic distribution of food. There was no panic. See in this the order I can bring to your life today.

Then Jesus directed them to have all the people sit down in groups on the green grass. So they sat down in groups of hundreds and fifties. Mark 6:39–40

Throughout the Day

Lord, help me to live a yielded life to You today.

TO BE MEEK, you must be willing to yield to My will for you at all times during the day. The frustrations you feel come not from outside circumstances, but from your reluctance to yield to Me throughout the day. You tend to be open to My will in your morning time with Me but reluctant to sense My will during the day. Be willing to turn to Me often. Rearrange your plans when I ask you to do so. Trust me with your plans and accept My will for you wholeheartedly in the big and small things in life, in the morning and throughout the day.

Three times a day he got down on his knees and prayed, giving thanks to his God, just as he had done before. Daniel 6:10

Decide to be Grateful

Lord, change my heart this morning.

MY SAVING GRACE cannot flow through a heart that is bitter and ungrateful. Decide to be grateful. Let Christ's power to save flow through you and impact others. Enjoy connecting with others. Have a warmer personality. Sow and reap where I send you. My ways are bountiful, bringing full harvest of choice fruit and grain. Decide to be grateful, and I can use you. Let each thank-you to Me raise your ability to show My grace to all around you.

I will give thanks to you, LORD, with all my heart; I will tell of all your wonderful deeds. Psalm 9:1

NOVEMBER 25 –
A Day of Celebration

Help me to be in step with Your Spirit today.

LET YOUR DAY be a day of celebration, a celebration of Me as a bright reality in your life, a celebration of those close to you and their importance in your life. Celebrate all the good you see in others. Celebrate spiritual gifts from the unseen: eternal life, love, joy, and peace. Celebrate My Spirit that is alive and well in you. Celebrate these gifts that are of more worth than all worldly possessions.

They celebrate your abundant goodness and joyfully sing of your righteousness. Psalm 145:7

Love Is Heaven's Currency

Help me to know more about You, Lord.

I AM CHANGING you from the inside out, pushing through you the spiritual currents of the Holy Spirit. You are a soul who resides in an earthly body. Your essence—who you really are—is spiritual. Unleash My power within you. My power is a weapon of love. The highest spiritual element is love. Against love and human warmth, Satan cannot stand. He retreats in sulking defeat against Heaven's mighty roar. Love is Heaven's currency, and it holds all true power. Love knocks down walls. Love recreates and reenergizes all. Love is Heaven spread down on the earth, a lifeline for the hurting, joy to the ragged, help for the jaded, hope for the depressed, and courage for the scarred. It is Heaven's currency.

Your love, LORD, reaches to the heavens, your faithfulness to the skies. Psalm 36:5

Influence Your World

Lord, let me spend my time being effective for You.

BROKENNESS IS HIDDEN deeply in the heart of man—the shame of disconnection from his earthly father and his heavenly Father. You have felt this as well. The great work is to be a peacemaker along with Me. It is the work of restoration. To believe you are making a difference in the lives of others is to feel joy. I am freeing up your schedule so you can work more and more for Me. Your story is explaining the freedom you have found by listening to only one voice. Influence your world. Act where I tell you to act. Have influence where I ask you to have influence.

Peacemakers who sow in peace reap a harvest of righteousness. James 3:18

God-Inspired Work

Jesus, thank You for Your care, love, and provision.
Help me feel Your security when I am uncertain.

LET GOD-INSPIRED WORK rule the day. Too much talk drains you. Strain out the dross in your day. To do more in a day than I intended for you to do damages the real work you were meant to do for Me. Learn to stop and pray before beginning a new conversation or task. Ask, "Lord, is this meant for me? Do you want me to do this?" Then, listen. I will respond. In so doing, you will gain a poise that will make your life a beacon for the kingdom. Seek the specific tasks I have assigned for you. When you do too much, you are not living a life built on grace and identity in Me.

When there are many words, transgression is unavoidable, but he who restrains his lips is wise. Proverbs 10:19 NASB

Meant to Feel Invincible

Thank You for Your protection for me and my family.

FEEL THE JOY that My protection brings to your life and family. I protect you from the guilt and shame that threaten to destroy your joy. My protection erases the fear of the future so that you can have the thrill of living in the present. Do not fret about the future of your children. They are protected as Our Father's children and as members of His family. My followers are meant to feel invincible, not because of any power of their own, but through My perpetual protection and saving grace. Let this joy lead you to worship.

For this reason I kneel before the Father, from whom every family in heaven and on earth derives its name. Ephesians 3:14–15

God's Spring in Your Step

Jesus, I am still bothered by the events of yesterday. Let me bring those to You so that you can lift them away from me.

A HOE FOR the plentiful garden. A Bible for a growing church. A freed heart for a powerful life. Thank Me for all, and talk with Me about all that bothers you. I am strong to carry your burdens. Too often you rush through your day, ignoring the pains and jolts of life. Be more childlike. Emotionally healthy children know when they have been hurt or frustrated; they do not ignore the pain. As your Father's son, be emotionally healthy. Stop and pray. Pause and turn to Me and Heaven. Plead your situation so that you do not keep the pain of the day within you. Share all with Me and then, in a moment, your pain is lifted, and you continue light and free with God's spring in your step.

Cast all your anxiety on him because he cares for you. 1 Peter 5:7

Greatest Finds in the World

Lord, help me have the right perspective on all this Christmas month.

LOVE. JOY. PEACE. These are the greatest finds in this world. These intangibles should be the hallmark of this time of year. Millions seek to recover glimpses of them during the holidays—perhaps seeking remembrances from their childhood—but find themselves still wanting all the more. Their search leaves them tired, nerve-strained, and stressed. Give to all the real gifts that are hidden in Me: love, joy, and peace.

The kingdom of heaven is like a merchant looking for fine pearls. When he found one of great value, he went away and sold everything he had and bought it. Matthew 13:45–46

DECEMBER 2 –

What a Life!

Lord, free me from all that hinders me from serving You completely.

BE A MORE sympathetic person. See the needs of others around you. Practice this active listening so I can use you and your wife marvelously. You must see a person's need to know how you can serve them. Oh, to be used to bring souls to Me in this way—what a life! Learn to read a person like a book, carefully gathering important information so that you can love them as I direct and guide you. God-led. God-blessed. Your level of sympathy toward others can be one of your greatest strengths.

All of this is from God, who reconciled us to himself through Christ and gave us the ministry of reconciliation. 2 Corinthians 5:18

DECEMBER 3 –

The Fruit of the Spirit Is Joy

Jesus, let me have the joy which can only come from above.

GIVE THE HOLY Spirit free reign in your life today. Let His heavenly promptings allow you to do good things and share good thoughts with others. Unselfish living brings joy. Do all with a smile—your confidence on display that all is well or will be made right because of My goodness. Let Me help you to see the joy in My life on the earth. It was with joy that I freed the woman of eighteen years of infirmity in her back. It was with joy that I received the good-hearted leper's words of thanks. It was with tears of joy that I raised dear Lazarus from the grave. It was with joy that I shared grace and truth with the Samaritan woman. Let joy be the note that is heard by others when you obey the Spirit's call.

On a Sabbath Jesus was teaching in one of the synagogues, and a woman was there who had been crippled by a spirit for eighteen years. She was bent over and could not straighten up at all. Luke 13:10–11

The Mystery of God

Jesus, I do not understand all the events of the last few days but give me a heart that worships You.

WESTERN MAN WOULD have all the mystery of life removed. But so often, God is in the mystery. It is good for man to know that he will never fully understand the mind of God and all the intricacies of the universe. It is good for man to know he is finite. It is healthy for man at times to feel powerless in the face of events. Draw near to Me this December. Simple worship. Simple obedience. Simple messages delivered. Worship the God you know, and live in wonder of the mysteries of His kingdom.

Beyond all question, the mystery from which true godliness springs is great. 1 Timothy 3:16

DECEMBER 5 –

Eternal Life Now

Lord, thank You for the promise of Heaven.

THE GREATEST GIFT from Heaven is eternal life. This life does not begin with a believer's death. It begins with the acceptance of all Heaven has to offer in this life. It begins when a soul takes the charge to follow Me as Lord and Savior and greets Me in the free waters of baptism. This gift transfigures your life today. To see eternal life in the correct perspective, focus on the quality of this life as well as its longevity. Life lived in My presence is available here and now, even if its fulfillment awaits in the afterlife. A full life, a meaningful life with Me, can be found in the present age. It is now that this life transfigures you. A life lived in My presence is a foretaste of Heaven. This meaningful life is available now. Enjoy a deep peace and sense of joy from this knowledge. You have this eternal life now.

I write these things to you who believe in the name of the Son of God so that you may know that you have eternal life. 1 John 5:13

An Adventurous Life

I am open to Your leading and guidance this morning. Jesus, help me to do all Your will for me.

THE FLORIDA EVERGLADES. Denali National Park. The Grand Canyon. These are adventurous locations full of excitement and fun. A man's heart craves adventure—fun connected with risk. Often doldrums are the enemy's weapons as much as worry, doubt, and guilt. I want to give you glad adventures with Me here and now. When you answer the call to follow Me, you sign up for a life of adventure as you serve Me. Say today, "Be quick to listen to Him."

He told them, "The harvest is plentiful, but the workers are few. Ask the Lord of the harvest, therefore, to send out workers into his harvest field." Luke 10:2

Pray in Complete Sentences

Lord, help me with this hurry sickness I feel this morning.

BE UNHURRIED IN all you do. I encourage you to linger with Me longer. The power of contact with Me as your friend and partner makes all life different. But to feel this connection, speak to me plainly in complete sentences. This will unleash the peace of mind I would have you feel. Your broken prayers to Me are symptoms of the rush and panic you feel. Speak to me in complete sentences. This will bring the leisurely pace into your day that commends the Christian life.

Do not be anxious about anything, but in every situation, by prayer and petition, with thanksgiving, present your requests to God. Philippians 4:6

Freedom to Serve

Jesus, provide joy for me today and bring meaning to my life.

LET ME SHOW you the way to real joy. I trust My followers. I do not attempt to control them. A Christian's walk is a free response to Heaven's warm love. Connect with Me as your great friend. Out of your gratitude for that friendship, serve Heaven. As a happy volunteer with Me for Heaven, you will find your joy. Do not allow sin or self to prevent service for Me, but also do not force work I am not calling you to. I seek joyful volunteers for Heaven's cause.

Therefore, since we receive a kingdom that cannot be shaken, let us show gratitude, by which we may offer to God an acceptable service with reverence and awe. Hebrews 12:28 NASB

DECEMBER 9 –
Perfect Peace

Lord, I need a miracle in my heart today.

PERFECT PEACE COMES from uniting with Me. Lies and half-truths surround the life of man. The devil uses guilt, fear, and shame to prompt many actions and reactions. Step aside with Me to this secret place in order to have abundant life. Heaven's aims for you are to bless you. Heaven replenishes and nourishes; the devil aims to exact a fearsome toll. Live for the kingdom and tell the devil to go back to hell.

Do not be afraid of those who kill the body but cannot kill the soul. Rather, be afraid of the One who can destroy both soul and body in hell. Matthew 10:28

Warmed by What Remains

Lord, thank You for this beautiful cardinal.

SOME BIRDS NEED to fly south for the winter; they have no warmth, no joy without My sun. The cardinal you see stays, warmed by what remains and his faith in the promised spring. Be warmed by what remains. Believe in your promised spring. Spiritually, spring can blossom in winter. Be warmed by My presence and the glad plans I have for your life. Live today in the warmth that remains.

The LORD turned to him and said, "Go in the strength you have and save Israel out of Midian's hand. Am I not sending you?" Judges 6:14

DECEMBER 11 –
Yielded Will

Thank You for the freedom and the peace of mind that comes from serving You and listening to Your voice.

YIELDING IN THE little things of life makes it easier to yield in the big things. If you are unwilling to yield in the small things, you will be unwilling to yield in the large things. Take on the spirit of meekness. Let soft and gentle meekness permeate your being. Be meek toward your God and those close to you. Learn the power of a yielded will. Learn this, and I can use you in greater ways.

Blessed are the meek, for they will inherit the earth. Matthew 5:5

Cleanse Your Mind

Lord, help me today to be clothed and in my right mind.

DO NOT ROB yourself of the sweet simplicity that faith can bring to your life. Make few plans for the future other than what you hear as My instructions for the day. All is well and going according to My plans for you. Bless Me with a trusting, childlike heart. Add righteousness to your life by trusting Me absolutely in all things. Let faith immediately lay to rest any temptation to overplan. Cleanse your mind from worry by specific, faithful prayer. Say, "The Lord will take care of all."

Therefore, I tell you do not worry about your life, what you will eat or drink; or about your body, what you will wear. Is not life more than food, and the body more than clothes? Matthew 6:25

DECEMBER 13 –
You Are Enough

Lord, I did not foresee what happened yesterday. Let me respond as a Christian.

I AM IN control of your life when all is blue skies and wonderful sunshine. I am also in control when there are thunderstorms and fierce lightening. I control all and will provide all you need in every situation. If you have a surprising turn of events in your life, especially if the turn is not what you wanted, know that it is not a surprise to Me. When gray days surround you and your heart sinks, look to Me and say, "Jesus, You are enough for me."

I say to myself, "The LORD is my portion; therefore I will wait for him." Lamentations 3:24

Noble Pursuits

Give me a new heart today and good things to do.

THE WORLD WANTS a superficial savior to rid itself from a variety of outward circumstances. But what man needs is a personal Savior to save him from inner struggles. This requires more superpower than the world can fathom. I came to save man from himself—his biggest obstacle. And, so with you. If left alone, you are mired in doubt, self-pity, and unworthy pursuits. But I save you from these. I make you new and spur you on to noble pursuits.

Finally, brothers and sisters, whatever is true, whatever is noble, whatever is right, whatever is pure, whatever is lovely, whatever is admirable—if anything is excellent or praiseworthy—think about such things.
Philippians 4:8

Heaven's Light

I pray for those who are suffering all around me.

EVIL ROAMS THE earth, but it does not run amok without restraint. Satan's darkness cannot withstand Heaven's light. Wherever Heaven's cast is permitted to shine, he shrinks back, powerless and defeated. Let My light shine brightly in and around you today. Be prepared to interject Heaven into the world. If necessary, say out loud, "Jesus' light is here with me."

Therefore do not be partners with them. For you were once darkness, but now you are light in the Lord. Live as children of light. Ephesians 5:7–8

Mercy, not Sacrifice

Lord, help me to do the things You would have me to do.

IF YOU FOCUS on your works, your mind dwells on sacrifice, self, and personal effort. Instead, focus on mercy and the Father's lavish love and kindness. Receive mercy in good measure so that you can give mercy and a sense of grace to others. Let grace cause joy, peace, and calm to bubble over and affect those around you. Believe in God's mercy for yourself and its availability to all. Be convinced that all is well because of the mercy extended to you. Then I can use you to help others.

But go and learn what this means: "I desire mercy, not sacrifice." For I have not come to call the righteous, but sinners. Matthew 9:13

Alone with Me

Lord, help me be the best Christlike version of me I can be.

COME BE ALONE with Me, not bound by any other relationships—away alone with Heaven, without influence from your earthly father, mother, siblings, friends, or even your wife. In this way, you can be true to Me. But even when you are freed from the demands and expectations of earthly relationships, there still remains the self. Self wants. Self desires. Self means and ends. See self as the enemy to be defeated. It must be a surrendered you who waits with Me. Achieve total victory over self so that God's beautifully made character can be revealed in you, layer by layer, day by day.

Anyone who loves their father or mother more than me is not worthy of me; anyone who loves their son or daughter more than me is not worthy of me.
Matthew 10:37

DECEMBER 18 —
All Planned

Lord, thank You for the path You have for me. I choose to enjoy You here and now.

SEE ME MORE in your day. See Me in nature all around you. See each of the day's events, each of its unfoldings, as specifically planned by Me to bless you and those you love. Leave it to the pagans to see the unfolding of their lives as haphazard, random, and void of love. Believe that every detail of your life is loving- ly planned by Me. Count your blessings for each mo- ment. Find My blessing for you in all the details. Even if events are painful, see them as beacons pulling you closer to Heaven and Heaven's will for you.

The Lord will watch over your coming and going both now and forevermore. Psalm 121:8

Whisper My Name

Jesus, let me hear Your voice today.

TOO MANY WORDS drown out My presence and the quiet voice that seeks to speak to you. Throughout your day, silently call on My name—"Jesus." Let us experience this day together. Let no problem with other people nor worry over money stand in Heaven's way for you. Whisper My name to remind you of your spiritual identity as God's son and My brother. All is well in My kingdom. The more you focus on spiritual values, the better you will understand yourself and your role in this world. Your job is to help expand that kingdom on earth. Your task is to open corners of earth to My influence. Listen to the Spirit's gentle promptings and then obey. Love. Help. Encourage. Whisper to yourself, "Jesus."

These are the things God has revealed to us by his Spirit. The Spirit searches all things, even the deep things of God. 1 Corinthians 2:10

Key to Success

Lord, forgive me for my mistakes.

THOUGH YOU FEEL personal failure, success for you is just around the corner. Trust My protection and guidance. Yes, it is a mistake to fail to follow My instructions. This hides the risen life from you. But I am a God of love and forgiveness, not anger and retribution. Feel My grace. Begin each day anew, ready to obey My promptings for you. Each day I show you a new path to follow. "I want to hear Him and obey"—this refrain is the key to your success. After you have applied the full balm of My grace, let these words refresh and revive you.

The steadfast love of the LORD never ceases; his mercies never come to an end; they are new every morning; great is your faithfulness. Lamentations 3:22–23 ESV

DECEMBER 21 –
Fight for Joy

Jesus, give me a heart that pleases You.

FIGHT FOR JOY this Christmas season. Say to yourself, "My Friend says all is well." Discharge your duties but also relax and be in a holiday mood. The world rushes by you. The world lacks inner peace and joy. Fight for joy by counting as loss all things compared to the value of knowing Me. Fight for joy by giving Me thanks for the other believers in your life. Surely, there is no mirth compared to the joy of My followers. All is well for you.

How can we thank God enough for you in return for all the joy we have in the presence of our God because of you. 1 Thessalonians 3:9

A Daily Walk

Jesus, help me to walk with You today, to do Your work, and to feel Your nearness and presence.

MAN NEEDS DAILY renewal. Thus, the need to walk *daily* with Me. You are learning that there is little carryover, spiritually speaking, from the day before. See yourself as a small child who must rely upon the caretaking of his kind father. This is a fitting picture of the dependent lifestyle intended for My followers. There is a joy to life that you must get up and obtain daily. Each day you must be kept safe, pure, and clean in Me. Walk in lockstep with Me today. The joy you seek will follow.

Therefore, whoever takes the lowly position of this child is the greatest in the kingdom of heaven. Matthew 18:4

A Time to Celebrate Miracles

Lord, I claim Your peace this Christmas season. Give me Your peace when I have little.

YOU FEEL STRANDED by the side of the road, your vehicle in disrepair. Your strength is that you have come to the right place. Here, with me, I interject joy, hope, and peace into your being. Christmas season is a time to celebrate miracles. My greatest miracles are in the unseen. Here, in your quiet time with Me, I perform a miracle in your heart. As you celebrate your Savior's birth, also celebrate the new life I breathe into your heart each day.

When they saw the star, they were overjoyed. On coming to the house, they saw the child with his mother Mary, and they bowed down and worshiped him. Then they opened their treasures and presented him with gifts of gold, frankincense and myrrh. Matthew 2:10–11

Fully Present

May Your will be done in my family this Christmas. Fill me this morning with those things that I do not have within me.

LEAVE ALL YOUR business concerns to Me today. Send those to Me to deal with one by one. Today and tomorrow are about family and worship. All is well even if things seem chaotic. Let loose of all that hinders you so that you can be fully present. Do this through your faith in My strength. Let your faith in My protection give you the courage to be a gentle soul to all you greet today.

Be strong and courageous, and do the work. Do not be afraid or discouraged, for the LORD God, my God, is with you. 1 Chronicles 28:20

DECEMBER 25 –
A Christmas Feast

Lord, bless our celebration this day of Your birth. Let Your love be present. I, too, kneel before the babe of Bethlehem and give You honor and praise.

IN MY DAYS on the earth, we celebrated Passover to remember the exodus and Pentecost to remember the gift of the law. My Christians gather on this Christmas Day to remember and celebrate My birth. Let the light that comes from the babe of Bethlehem shine brightly for all today. Clear the clutter from your mind. Feast today on the Father's best gift to man: a loving Savior who allows everyone to come home. Bring glory to Heaven today by celebrating the birth that still changes the world.

Today in the town of David a Savior has been born to you; he is the Messiah, the Lord. Luke 2:11

The Wonderful Counselor

Meet me here this morning, Jesus.

MAN FAILS TO comprehend that inner peace cannot be achieved by reasoning. Only I understand each heart and mind. A wise guide points others to Me, the Wonderful Counselor who can provide personal counseling to all. Man needs to hear and see Me, and then all is well; he is then dressed and in his right mind. Ask for listening ears to catch Heaven's message for you and eyes that can see the path I have for you. Be wary of those who parade as learned and wise when in earnest they are fakes and posers, blind guides to My lost sheep. A daily walk with Me is truly the cure for all ills. Wise men seek Me and point others to Me.

For to us a child is born, to us a son is given, and the government will be on his shoulders. And he will be called Wonderful Counselor, Mighty God, Everlasting Father, Prince of Peace. Isaiah 9:6

The Solution to All Problems

Jesus, come strengthen me and make me whole.

I AM THE temple that makes the gold sacred. Only in Me can Heaven's highest creation find its worth. I am the solution to all of man's problems. I am the caulk for each crack and the plug for each hole. I am the salve for mankind and the remedy for each man's malady. Exhortations about Me are not hyperbole because I am all that man truly needs. Say today, "I have Jesus; I have all I need."

Which is greater, the gold or the temple that makes the gold sacred? Matthew 23:17

The Calm Voice

Lord, I pray today to be a humble man. Help me to have a humble spirit.

LOUD AND ANGRY voices never bring My success. Spiritual steps are taken by hearing the calm voice that speaks to you. That voice always has the best intentions for you and those around you. Let Me gently speak to you and guide your steps. Together, we move down the right path that will also be a blessing for others. Let Me give to you so that you can give to others. I soothe the nerves frayed by the hectic pace of the world. I bind the wounds inflicted by the evil one. Say to yourself today, "The meek shall inherit the earth and win the day."

But the meek will inherit the land and enjoy peace and prosperity. Psalm 37:11

DECEMBER 29 –

Protect You from Yourself

Lord, help me to clear my mind and think straight.

CONTACT WITH ME brings healing. This contact is the salt that purifies and protects your soul. I remove thoughts from your mind that do not advance your soul's best interest. I pour a full dose of grace on your fears of not measuring up to the man you think you should be. Here I protect you from yourself. One of My Christian's greatest gifts is the ability to see himself as I see him: redeemed and risen with Me, fully accepted and embraced. You can leave your time spent with Me whole and happy. Your Master brings Heaven to earth.

But I have prayed for you, Simon, that your faith may not fail. And when you have turned back, strengthen your brothers. Luke 22:32

DECEMBER 30 –

Stand and Believe

Lord, what are You doing? Where are You moving?

YOU SEE THE storm rage against your home. You hear the wind and waves, and the noise is deafening. But your path is clear: stand and believe. All that happens in your life is linked. All is connected. All the good I have planned for you will unfold at the right time. I am never slow to act and am never deaf to your prayers. You must trust completely that I am good and will bring good to you and those near you. Say today, "I will stand today and believe My friend is good."

The Lord is not slow in keeping his promises, as some understand slowness. Instead he is patient with you, not wanting anyone to perish, but everyone to come to repentance. 2 Peter 3:9

Heaven's Personality

*As another year ends and a new one begins, let me
have a mind-set that pleases You.*

YOU HAVE AN old man inside of you whom I wish
to move out of the way. He does not have My purposes
for you in mind. The kingdom is a place of growth, renewal, and youth. You can be the youngest man in any
room by the power of My Spirit that fills you with hope
for the future and joy in your work for Me. This is the
right kingdom mind-set. It is one full of hope and joy;
it is Heaven's personality.

Truly I tell you, unless you change and become like little children, you will never enter the kingdom of heav-
en. Matthew 18:3

AFTERWORD
Suggestions for Quiet Listening

I DO NOT presume to instruct you how to have a quiet time because connecting with Him is a personal matter for each Christ-follower. I share here only what has been beneficial for me. Nor do I attempt to cover other important parts of my own quiet time like Bible reading and Scripture memorization. Instead, I offer here a few tips for those who would like to try quiet listening. To some, the proposition that the Lord can speak to us is somewhat sensational, maybe even heretical. In my view, the New Testament attests to the power of God to reconnect with His children. In the Old Testament, the curtain of the temple demonstrated the limitation of God's children to enter His presence. Jesus' obedience on the cross tore the curtain in two, signifying our ability to gain full access to God. If the power of the cross grants access to the presence of God, I think it is reasonable that we seek His presence daily and be changed by what we receive and hear in His company.

1. **Journaling**. In our prayer life, we often make the same mistake with the Lord as with our friends: we do all the talking. James 1:19 states in part that, "Everyone should be quick to listen and slow to speak." We know that this Scripture applies to our earthly friendships, but it should also apply to our relationship with Jesus. As the saying goes: the Lord gave us two ears and one mouth to show us that we should listen twice as much as we speak. If you are wondering how a person tries the practice of quiet listening, the answer is, you write. A rudder cannot steer a boat at rest; you must jump in and begin. There is a value to placing our prayers in writing; I know of no better way of catching the Lord's message for our lives. As some have said, the palest ink is stronger than the best memory. Write whatever comes to your mind: good things, odd things, and stray thoughts. Not everything you write will be from the Lord, but write to make the connection with Him. Write until you feel that it is His voice speaking to you. Write until you feel there is an ending to the message. You may write down a spiritual thought about a Scripture you have read or some assurance for a worry you have. You may have

a prompting to apologize to someone, a name may come to you of someone you should call for lunch, or you may receive insight into a personal problem.

2. **Checking what you have written**. As protection against being led astray by a whim or errant message, we should check what we have written. Jesus will never prompt any action or decision that is contrary to the Bible. Like the Bereans in Acts 17, we should eagerly examine the Scriptures daily to make sure what we hear is true to orthodox belief. As a shorthand method of checking what we have written, we should ask if it is absolutely *loving, pure, honest,* and *unselfish*. In the words of Jesus' half-brother, heavenly wisdom "is first of all pure; then peace-loving, considerate, submissive, full of mercy and good fruit, impartial and sincere" (James 3:17).

3. **Cultivating silence**. In this age, the command to "be still, and know that I am God" (Psalm 46:10) may be one of the most difficult Scriptures for us to obey. Our world beckons us to be continually busy and yokes us with a kind of hurried sickness.

There is no substitute for the self-discipline of waiting on the Lord. We should be content to sit with Him even if He has no words for us. Being in His presence changes us, heals us, and makes us whole.

4. **Hearing Jesus' voice**. As Christians, we worship the God in tripart: the Father, the Son, and the Holy Spirit. However, in my personal prayer time, I talk to Jesus and listen for His voice. The Lord said when He was on the earth that to know Him is to know the Father. And since, in Jesus, we have a personal Savior who knows all our struggles and who Himself was tempted in every way, it makes sense to me to talk to Him in my quiet times. In silence, I then give Him an opportunity, through the Holy Spirit, to share what He will with me.

5. **Using earplugs**. It is almost too trite a thing to mention the use of earplugs, but I suppose this is an important enough aspect of my quiet time that I add it here. After I have read and before I begin my prayer time, I insert soft foam earplugs. This practice affords me greater concentration, and I am

less likely to be distracted. I encourage you to try it for yourself.

6. **Using index cards**. In my journal, I keep a supply of index cards. I do this for two reasons. First, whenever I get up in the morning, I inevitably have to-do things rush at me. I write these down on my index card for the day so that I can get them out of my head, and so I will not forget to do them later. Secondly, I use the index card as a way of carrying my quiet time with me into the day. I write the spiritual thought of the day on the top of the card that may be a Scripture or, as shown in a number of my entries in this book, a phrase or prayer. Keeping this refrain in my mind throughout the day allows me to control what I think and extends my quiet time in a way I hope makes me a saltier Christian. I also write any promptings I may have heard. These are the things I want to obey in my day. These are usually associated with people but can also be other things like fresh insight into a problem in our home or that I may have at work.

7. **Obedience**. We often speak of someone accepting Jesus or praying Him into his or her heart as a way of indicating their first introduction to our great Friend. However, the Bible speaks in terms of a new believer making Him their Lord and Savior and *following Him*. I believe through the practice of quiet listening our Lord carries out the Great Commission through us in a way that moves us from human-based effort to work inspired by Heaven. In this regard, I think that there are two stages of a believer's obedience. The first is when we make the Bible the standard for our lives and use our best efforts to hold to it. The second is when we are also willing to follow His promptings to us individually. This second stage of obedience is when our Christian faith becomes a real adventure as we follow the living Christ who passionately wants to change the world every day. The Lord knows far better than we do who around us is in need or who may be most open to taking that next step toward Him. In my own life, there have been times when I have received a prompting to reach out to a person only to find that it was the perfect timing for that person to turn to Him. I am convinced that the Lord

desires to use us in this way as we partner with Him to help His hurting world.

Order Information

To order additional copies of this book, please visit
www.redemption-press.com.
Also available on Amazon.com and BarnesandNoble.com
or by calling toll free 1-844-2REDEEM.

CPSIA information can be obtained
at www.ICGtesting.com
Printed in the USA
BVHW030153150820
586505BV00001B/1